DESERT *Treasures*

Culinary Creations from the Valley of the Sun

The Junior League of Phoenix

COVER DESCRIPTION:

Overflowing with the bounty of the Sonoran Desert, a hammered silver chest holds the freshest ingredients for Treasures' cuisine.

Familiar citrus, tomatoes, and grapes join the sacred Indian triad of corn, squash, and beans, and complement lesser-known tomatillo, pomegranate, and prickly pear.

First Edition   First Printing   40,000 copies

ISBN 0-9613174-1-8

Printed in the USA by
WIMMER BROTHERS
A Wimmer Company
Memphis • Dallas

PURPOSE OF THE JUNIOR LEAGUE OF PHOENIX

The Junior League of Phoenix is an organization of women committed to promoting voluntarism and to improving the community through the effective action and leadership of trained volunteers. Its purpose is exclusively educational and charitable.

The profits realized from the sale of **Desert Treasures** will be used by the Junior League of Phoenix, Inc., to support the projects it sponsors in the community.

Additional copies of **Desert Treasures** may be obtained by writing:

> Desert Treasures
> P.O. Box 10223
> Phoenix, Arizona 85064

Please enclose your return address with a check payable to Junior League of Phoenix in the amount of $18.95 plus $2.50 in postage and handling for one book and $5.00 for two or more books.

Committee

CHAIRMEN
Rebecca Baker
Susie Wisz

EDITOR
Lyn Fairfax

TESTING CHAIRMEN
Marsha Dyer
Sue Harris

MARKETING
Ann Brown

INDEX
Gail Creasman

WRITER
Linda Teichgraeber

UNDERWRITING
Beth Carson

RESORT AND RESTAURANT
RECIPES
Michelle Felker

DESIGN
Jennifer Sands

SALES
Carole Moreno

ADVISORS
Michelle Felker
Rona Kasen

TREASURER
Evonne Bowling

DESIGN COMMITTEE

PHOTOGRAPHY SET DESIGN
Sharron Saffert
PHOTOGRAPHY
Ellen Maureen Urick
GRAPHIC ARTIST
Diane Young

ADMINISTRATIVE SUPPORT
Barbara Armstrong
Keven Matthew
Judy Stewart

The design of this book was created and produced by members of
The Junior League of Phoenix.

FINAL TASTING COMMITTEE

Rebecca Baker
Sandra Barnes
Kathy Bates
Sue Boyd
Anita Calihan
Karen Campbell
Tibby Cornelius
Robyn Dependahl
Marsha Dyer
Ann Fabric-Engle
Lyn Fairfax
Michelle Felker
Polly Fitz-Gerald
Vicki Granberry
Sue Harris
Gayle Holmgren
Nancy Hurley
Suzi Iliff
Rona Kasen
Claudia Neal
Linda Teichgraeber
Karen Vivian
Lyn Wiley
Susie Wisz

Acknowledgements

Desert Treasures Committee gives special recognition to the following individuals for their outstanding contributions to the production of this book.

Barbara Colleary
of
Culinary Creations

Cookie Levine
of
Levine Linens

William J. Martin
Chairman
of
Art/Photography Department
Scottsdale Community College

Dedications

The Junior League of Phoenix graciously acknowledges the
financial support it has received for the production of
Desert Treasures.

The chapter, Fiesta Favorites, is dedicated to the sustainers
of the Junior League of Phoenix, for the encouragement
and assistance which they have so generously given over
the past two years.

In memory of our grandparents,
Louis M. Sands and Frances P. Sands
who began their family's production of cattle
and farm products in Arizona in 1904.
Marilyn F. Harris
Charles F. Sands
Louis Sands, IV

Table of Contents

Introduction

The Junior League of Phoenix proudly presents **Desert Treasures**, a culinary creation from the Valley of the Sun. On the pages that follow, we offer not only our treasured recipes, but also the treasures of our geographical and cultural heritage.

Developed as a fund-raiser for the League, sales of **Desert Treasures** will empower our community projects with the dollars needed for success.

Founded in 1935, the Junior League of Phoenix has been enriching the lives of Phoenix citizens for 57 years. The League has continually emphasized issues and sponsored projects which affect the environment, the arts, and all community members, especially children.

Impacting the community with the proven partnership of funds coupled with the leadership skills of trained volunteers, the League has indeed made a difference.

The Junior League of Phoenix graciously thanks those who purchase **Desert Treasures**. Your purchase will assist young people who need the support of an outreach program, help women struggling against homelessness, and aid in the renovation of a landmark theatre in downtown Phoenix. Your support enables the League to remain united in its purpose—responsive to community need.

CURRENT COMMUNITY PROJECTS

Arizona Foundation Directory
Emily Anderson Family Learning Center
Metropolitan Canal
Orpheum Theatre
Teen Outreach Program
Transitional Housing for the Homeless
YWCA/JLP Women In Transition

PAST COMMUNITY PROJECTS

Adult Illiteracy
Crisis Nursery
Junior Museum/Phoenix Art Museum
Museum of Science & Technology
Phoenix Zoo Education Center
Ronald McDonald House
Rosson House

Entertaining

Picnic in the Desert

Coyote Caviar   Apricot Pecan Canapes

Marinated Mushroom and Cauliflower Salad

Spicy Baby Back Ribs

Green Chili Corn Bread

Carrot Cookies   Mixed Nut Bars

Evening under the Stars

Phyllo Blossoms

Carrot Tarragon Soup

Hearts of Palm Salad with Tangy Lemon Dressing

Turkey with Raspberry Sauce

Herbed Asparagus

Rice Pecan Casserole

Unbelieveably Smooth and Creamy Cheesecake

Poolside Brunch

Cold Cucumber Tomato Soup

Brunch Bake with Sun Dried Tomatoes

Oaxacan Fruit Salad

Frozen Berry Chiffon

Phoenix Style

Backyard Barbecue

Quick Chili Relleno Dip

Grilled Margarita Chicken

Chilled Herbed Tomatoes

Picante Corn Casserole

Fresh Herb Butter on French Bread

Lemon Blueberry Mousse

Artwalk Supper

Paloma Plantation Pecans

Caesar Salad

Spedini Alla Romona

Lemon Sours   Chocolate Mint Squares

Christmas in the Southwest

Warm Goat Cheese With Sun Dried Tomatoes

Squash Bisque

Colorful Black Bean Salad

Fiesta Corn Tamale Torte

with

Salsa Fresca

Fresh Fruit

Cranberry Pie

appetizers

Goat Cheese Torte

8 ounces cream cheese
8 ounces Goat cheese
3 sticks butter, softened

1 cup pesto
1 cup sun dried tomatoes,
  drained and minced

- Beat the cheeses and butter until well blended and fluffy.
- Fill small springform pan (or any decorative bowl) with ⅓ of the cheese mixture followed by ½ of the pesto. Repeat.
- Cover with last portion of cheese mixture and spread tomatoes on top.
- Refrigerate at least one hour.
- Serve at room temperature with sliced baguettes or crackers.
  Serves 12-16.

Coyote Caviar

A very Southwestern appetizer, and is sure to be a hit.

1 can (15 ounces) black beans,
  rinsed and drained
1 can (4 ounces) chopped ripe
  olives, drained
1 small onion, chopped
4 ounces diced green chilies
1 clove garlic, chopped
4 tablespoons cilantro,
  chopped
2 tablespoons vegetable oil
2 tablespoons lime juice

2 teaspoons chili powder
¼ teaspoon salt
¼ teaspoon crushed red pepper
¼ teaspoon cumin
1 teaspoon pepper
1 package (8 ounces) cream
  cheese, softened
2 hard boiled eggs, peeled and
  chopped
1 green onion, sliced
salsa

- Mix all ingredients EXCEPT cream cheese, eggs, green onions, and salsa. Cover and refrigerate 2 hours.
- Spread cream cheese on round serving plate.
- Spoon bean mixture evenly over cream cheese.
- Arrange eggs on bean mixture around edges along with salsa. Sprinkle with green onions.
- Serve with tortilla chips.
  Serves 12.

Caviar Pie

15 hardboiled eggs, finely
  chopped
3 tablespoons mayonnaise
½ cup green onion, finely
  chopped

18 ounces cream cheese
3 tablespoons sour cream
4.5 ounces Servuga caviar

- Mix eggs and mayonnaise together. Place in bottom of 10" spring-form pan.
- Add onions on top of egg mixture.
- Mix cream cheese and sour cream together. Frost on top of onions.
- Refrigerate overnight. Before serving place caviar on top.
  Serves 8-12.

Pecan Apricot Canapé

1 package (6 ounces) dried
  apricots
40 pecan halves
1 package (8 ounces) cream
  cheese

2 tablespoons green onion,
  finely minced
¼ teaspoon salt
¼ teaspoon garlic salt
¼ cup fresh parsley, finely
  minced

- Toast pecan halves in skillet over low heat of 10 minutes, turning frequently. Cool and sprinkle with salt.
- Blend cream cheese, garlic salt, and green onions in a small bowl.
- Spread mixture on apricot half and press pecan on each.
- Roll edges in minced parsley.
  Serves 20.

Parmesan and Artichoke Rounds

¾ cup mayonnaise
¾ cup Parmesan cheese,
  grated
½ teaspoon onion juice
1 can (4 ounces) hearts of
  artichokes in water

tube of Pillsbury Snowflake
  Rolls or Hungry Jack Flaky
  Biscuits (10 ounces)
paprika

- Divide rolls into 36 sections and place on teflon cookie sheet.
- Mix mayonnaise, cheese and onion juice in a bowl. Spread on each dough section.
- Place a slice of artichoke heart on top of each section. Top with more mayonnaise mixture. Sprinkle with paprika.
- Bake at 400° for 10-12 minutes.
  Serves 12-18.

Vegetable Tart

1 package refrigerated pie
  crust
2 cups blanched broccoli, cut
  in small pieces
2 cups blanched cauliflower,
  cut in small pieces
2 cups blanched carrots, cut in
  small pieces

8 eggs, beaten
2 teaspoons milk or half and
  half
¼ cup Parmesan cheese, grated
salt and pepper to taste
1 egg yolk, lightly beaten

- Lay one pie crust in 8" or 9" square pan. Arrange vegetables on crust.
- Mix beaten eggs with milk, and carefully pour over vegetables.
- Sprinkle vegetable and eggs with Parmesan cheese. Add salt and pepper to taste.
- Place second pastry piece on top and crimp edges. Brush top with egg yolk and prick pastry with fork.
- Bake at 350-375° for 40 minutes until golden brown.
- Let set 5-10 minutes before cutting into small squares for appetizer.
  Serves 8.

Guacamole Chili Chips

2 large ripe avocados, peeled
  and mashed
3 tablespoons lemon juice
2 tablespoons onion, grated
1 tablespoon mayonnaise
2 teaspoons yellow mustard
½ teaspoon salt
¼ teaspoon Tabasco

1 large bag of tortilla chips (14
  ounces)
½ pound Monterey Jack
  cheese, shredded
1 jar (12 ounces) green chili
  salsa
1 cup sour cream

- Combine avocados, lemon juice, onion, mayonnaise, mustard, salt and Tabasco together.
- Place chips evenly on a cookie sheet and sprinkle with shredded cheese.
- Drizzle with salsa and place under broiler just to melt cheese.
- Break chips apart and place on serving plate. Top each chip with guacamole and sour cream.
- Serve immediately.
  Serves 8-12.

Stuffed Brie

1 round (4½ ounces) Brie
  cheese
1 package (3 ounces) cream
  cheese

3 tablespoons Blue cheese,
  crumbled
1-2 tablespoons dry sherry
⅛ cup almonds, sliced
¼ cup grapes, sliced

Looks beautiful on a tray filled with assorted crackers and lots of fresh red and green grapes.

- Slice Brie in half, like a hamburger bun.
- Mix cream cheese, sherry and Blue cheese until soft (it will still be lumpy).
- Add almonds and grapes to mixture, reserving a few for garnish.
- Spread mixture on top of Brie halves and garnish with almonds and grapes. Cut in wedges.
  Serves 6-8.

Jalapeño Cheddar Canapés

*1 cup extra sharp Cheddar
  cheese, grated*
1 large egg, lightly beaten

*2½ teaspoons pickled jalapeño
  peppers, minced*
*1 loaf thin sliced white bread
  (1 pound)*

- Cut out bread shapes with doughnut cutter or fancy canapé cutters.
- Place bread shapes on a cookie sheet and bake in a 250 degree oven until lightly toasted.
- Mix the remaining ingredients and spoon onto the toasts.
- Place under broiler about 4" from the heat for 2-3 minutes until puffed and golden.
  Serves 12.

Tomato Parmesan Gems

*You can also add
fresh or dried
basil on tomatoes
for an additional
flavor.*

2 tablespoons olive oil
1 clove garlic, minced
*8 Roma tomatoes or 4 regular
  tomatoes, sliced ½"*

24 sliced toasted baguettes
*1¼ cup fresh Parmesan cheese,
  grated*

- Sauté garlic in oil for 2 minutes.
- Add tomatoes to oil for 1 minute on each side.
- Place slices of tomato on each slice of bread.
- Place on cookie sheet and top with Parmesan.
- Broil 3 minutes and serve.
  Serves 8-10.

Pot Stickers

1 pound wonton skins
1½ pound ground beef
3-4 tablespoons soy sauce
1 teaspoon potato starch

*2 boxes (10 ounces) frozen
  spinach, defrosted, drained
  and chopped*
1 tablespoon sesame oil
2 tablespoons vegetable oil

- Combine beef, soy sauce, starch, spinach and sesame oil. Shape in a small ball and wrap in wonton skins.
- Cook in wok with 2 tablespoons vegetable oil for 5 minutes. Splash with 2 tablespoons water.
- Cover and cook 5-7 minutes.
- Serve with soy sauce and wine vinegar.
  Serves 6.

Phyllo Blossoms

Phyllo Dough

Southwest Filling:
¼ cup Cheddar cheese, grated
¼ cup Monterey Jack cheese, grated

Mushroom Filling:
¼ cup fresh mushrooms, chopped
½ tablespoon butter
⅓ cup cream cheese, softened

Chinese Vegetable Filling:
½ cup broccoli flowerettes
⅓ cup carrots, minced
1 tablespoon butter

Shrimp Filling:
⅓ cup baby shrimp
¼ cup sour cream
¼ cup cream cheese, softened

Apricot-Brie Filling:
1 small Brie

Butter, melted

2 tablespoons chopped green chilies or ½ tablespoon fresh jalapeños

2 tablespoons green onions, sliced
⅛ teaspoon garlic salt

2 tablespoons green onions, chopped
2 tablespoons bamboo shoots
1 tablespoon soy sauce

2 teaspoons dill weed
lemon juice

3 teaspoons apricot preserves

Easy to adapt to any party theme.

- Remove three sheets of phyllo dough at a time. Brush the top and bottom sheets with butter. (Be careful not to let the other sheets dry out.)
- Cut into 3X3 inch squares. Fit into small (1½-2") buttered muffin tins.
- Fill with your favorite filling. Bake at 350° for 10 minutes.

Southwest Filling:
- Mix all the ingredients together.

Mushroom Filling:
- Sauté the mushrooms in the butter. Add cream cheese to mushrooms, then the onions and garlic salt.

Chinese Vegetable Filling:
- Sauté broccoli and carrots in butter. Add green onions, bamboo shoots, and soy sauce.

Shrimp Filling:
- Mix all ingredients together.

Apricot-Brie Filling:
- Cut Brie into 6 small pieces. Place in 6 muffin cups. Top with ½ teaspoon apricot preserves.

Each filling mixture fills 6 muffin tins.

Warm Goat Cheese and Sun Dried Tomatoes

Serve with cored, chilled tart green apple wedges or thin slices of French bread.

Marinated sun dried tomatoes can be made by reconstituting dried, sun dried tomatoes and then marinating them in olive oil.

Canned, drained artichoke hearts make an interesting substitution.

1 log (11 ounces) Goat cheese
¼ cup plain dry breadcrumbs
3 tablespoons extra virgin olive oil, divided
1 teaspoon fresh garlic, minced
1 teaspoon fresh thyme, minced

pinch freshly ground pepper
3 tablespoons marinated sun dried tomatoes, chopped
green apples or French bread slices

- Spread Goat cheese in bottom of shallow 2 quart casserole.
- Mix the bread crumbs, 2 tablespoons of olive oil, thyme, garlic, and pepper together in a small bowl.
- Add the tomatoes and sprinkle over the cheese.
- Spread the bread crumb mixture over the cheese and tomatoes.
- Drizzle the remaining tablespoon of olive oil over top.
- At this point, the spread may be refrigerated until the next day, covered.
- Preheat oven to 375° and bake uncovered 10-12 minutes until heated through.
  Serves 10.

Devilled Almonds with Cheese

1 tablespoon black olives, minced
1 tablespoon Gherkin pickles, minced
1 tablespoon bottled chili sauce
1 teaspoon French's mustard

1 teaspoon Worcestershire sauce
1 cup almonds, blanched and finely chopped
1 tablespoon butter
cream cheese
salt and paprika to taste
melba toast rounds

- Mix olives, Gherkins and chili sauce in a bowl. Add mustard and Worcestershire sauce.
- Sauté almonds in butter until brown. Dust almonds with a little salt and paprika. Add to the devilled mixture.
- Frost tops of melba toast rounds with cream cheese and dip into almond mixture.
  Serves 12.

Hot Crabmeat Spread

1 package (8 ounces) cream
  cheese
2 tablespoons mayonnaise
4 tablespoons dry white wine
  or sherry

garlic salt to taste
1 teaspoon prepared mustard
2 teaspoons onion juice
dash seasoned salt
1 can (10¾ ounces) crabmeat

- Cream cheese, mayonnaise, wine, and all seasonings together.
- Flake crabmeat and fold into mayonnaise mixture. Do not use a beater.
- Heat in double boiler and serve hot in a chafing dish.
- Serve with cracker or rounds of toasted party ryes.
  Serves 20.

Shrimp Butter Spread

12 ounces fresh cooked shrimp,
  deveined, drained, and
  chopped
½ cup finely chopped onions

¼ pound real butter, softened
4 tablespoons mayonnaise
1 package (8 ounces) cream
  cheese

*Great dip served
with bagel chips.*

*Try using crab as
a change of pace.*

- Beat mayonnaise and cream cheese until fluffy.
- Slowly add butter to cheese and mayonnaise mixture.
- Add remaining ingredients and chill.
- Set out 20 minutes before serving.
  Serves 8.

Monterey Cheese Spread

2 pounds Monterey Jack
   cheese, grated
1 can (4 ounces) diced green
   chiles
1 can (4¼ ounces) chopped
   ripe olives

4 tomatoes, chopped
1 small bunch green onion,
   chopped
¼ cup fresh parsley, chopped
1 bottle (8 ounces) good Italian
   dressing

- Mix all ingredients together. Best if made ahead so flavors can blend.
- Serve with wheat thins, bagel chips, or tortilla chips.
  Serves 24.

French Herb Cheese Spread

Can be spread on a loaf of french bread and broiled in oven. Also great served on baked potatoes in place of sour cream.

1 package (8 ounces) cream
   cheese, softened
½ cup butter or margarine,
   softened
1 ounce Parmesan cheese,
   grated

2 tablespoons dry white wine
2 tablespoons fresh parsley,
   finely chopped
1 garlic clove, minced
⅛ teaspoon pepper
dash ground thyme

- Using an electric mixer, combine cream cheese and butter until well blended.
- Add rest of ingredients and mix till smooth.
- Chill at least 4 hours.
  Serves 8-10.

Quick Chili Relleno Dip

1 package (8 ounces) Monterey
Jack cheese, grated
1 package (8 ounces) Cheddar
or Colby cheese, grated

1 can (4 ounces) diced green
chiles
2 eggs, beaten
½ cup sour cream

Serve this dip hot or cold. Great with tortilla chips and accompanied with salsa.

- Preheat oven to 350°.
- Layer cheese and chiles in small, ungreased baking dish.
- Combine sour cream and eggs, and pour over it.
- Bake approximately 30 minutes. It will brown a little on top and appear custardy.
- Let sit 5 minutes before serving.
  Serves 10-12.

Greek Delight

1 pound Feta cheese, sliced
and halved
½ pound black olives
1 loaf French bread, sliced and
halved

2 cups olive oil
4 sun dried tomatoes, finely
chopped
2 tablespoons fresh oregano,
minced

- Marinate tomatoes in olive oil.
- Add 2 tablespoons fresh oregano.
- Let stand overnight.
- Dip bread into the olive oil, placing cheese and olive on top.
  Serves 12-16.

Better Than Boursin

16 ounces softened cream
  cheese
¼ cup mayonnaise
2 teaspoons Dijon mustard

2 tablespoons fresh chives,
  finely chopped
2 tablespoons fresh dill, finely
  chopped
1 clove garlic, minced

- Beat all ingredients with electric mixer until thoroughly blended.
- Spoon into a small serving bowl or into a two cup foil lined mold. Cover.
- Refrigerate overnight.
- Turn out on a small serving plate and peel off foil.
- Serve with crackers for spreading.
  Serves 8-12.

Pizza Pizzaz

Serve with your favorite crackers.

1 package (8 ounces) cream
  cheese, softened
½ cup sour cream
½ teaspoon garlic powder
½ cup pizza sauce

½ cup chopped pepperoni
¼ cup onion, chopped
¼ cup green pepper, chopped
½ cup Mozzarella cheese,
  shredded

- Mix cream cheese, sour cream, and garlic powder in a small bowl.
- Spread evenly in a 9 or 10 inch pie plate.
- Top with pizza sauce and sprinkle on pepperoni, onion, and green pepper.
- Bake in a 350° oven for 10 minutes.
- Top with Mozzarella cheese and bake an additional 5 minutes or until cheese is melted and pizza is hot throughout.
  Serves 12.

Skewered Pecan Chicken

*1 pound cooked chicken
  breasts, boned, skinned, bite-
  sized cubes*
½ cup dried apricots
3 tablespoons yellow mustard

*3 tablespoons Grey Poupon
  mustard*
3 tablespoons honey
1½ cups crushed pecans

*Try using various
nuts and dried
fruits for variety.*

- Blend mustard and honey in a small bowl.
- Thread chicken cube onto colored wooden toothpicks and dip into mustard sauce mixture. Let excess drip off.
- Dip cubes into nuts, coating evenly.
- Thread a small piece of dried fruit onto toothpick.
  Serves 24.

Chicken Cheese Rolls

*3 large chicken breasts, boned
  and split*
*8 ounces whipped cream
  cheese with chives*

*1 tablespoon butter or
  margarine, divided*
6 slices bacon

- Place split breasts between waxed paper and pound to ½ inch thickness.
- Spread each with 2 tablespoons cheese mixture and dot with ½ teaspoon butter.
- Fold ends over filling.
- Wrap one slice of bacon around each roll and place seam side down in shallow baking pan.
- Bake on top rack at 400° for 40 minutes or until chicken is tender and juices run clear when meat is pierced.
- Broil an additional 5 minutes or until bacon is crisp and golden.
- Slice into bite-sized pieces.
  Serves 12-16.

Tailgate Deli

Don't worry if it bursts while baking. This bread can be served immediately or wrapped in foil and frozen. Reheat at 250° for 30 minutes.

1 loaf frozen bread dough, thawed for 2-3 hours
1 package of sliced salami (6 ounces)
4 eggs

½ cup Parmesan cheese, grated
½ cup Monterey Jack cheese, grated
1 teaspoon oregano
1 teaspoon parsley

- Divide risen dough in half, and pat out into 4 x 10 pan.
- Place ½ of salami on each piece of dough leaving 1" clear all around edges.
- Beat eggs, Parmesan and spices together. Spoon some over salami, being careful not to let it run off.
- Cover with Jack cheese.
- Roll up long edge, seal short edges, and place seam down on greased cookie sheet.
- Brush loaf with remaining egg mixture.
- Bake at 350 ° for 25 minutes.
- Slice and serve.
  Serves 6-8.

Boboli Extravaganza

½ cup mayonnaise
1 teaspoon dried dill weed
2 cloves garlic, minced
¼ cup parsley, minced
⅛ teaspoon cayenne pepper
1 package (8 ounces) imitation crab
1 cup Cheddar cheese, shredded

1 cup Monterey Jack cheese, shredded
1 can (12¼ ounces) sliced black olives
1 can (14 ounces) artichoke hearts or bottoms, chopped
1 large Boboli bread

- Combine all ingredients except bread.
- Warm the bread for 5 minutes in 250° oven.
- Spread mixture on bread and broil for 3-4 minutes until cheese is melted.
  Serves 10-12.

Ceviche

2 generous pounds of red
   snapper, cut in 1x2" pieces
1½ cups fresh lime juice
1¼ cups water
2 medium white onions, pureed

4 cloves garlic, pureed
3 bay leaves
1 sprig thyme
1 sprig marjoram

Sauce:

12 black peppercorns, crushed
2 tablespoons oregano
½ tablespoon thyme
5 fresh chilies Serranos, finely
   chopped
½ tablespoon coriander seed
dash of ground cinnamon

1½ cups olive oil
4 cloves garlic, pureed
½ tablespoon cumin seed
1 pound mushrooms, sliced
1½ cups cilantro, chopped
2 cups stuffed olives
¾ cup capers

- Marinate fish overnight in water, lime juice, onion, garlic, bay leaf, thyme, and marjoram.
- Mix all the ingredients for the sauce in a bowl, adding mushrooms, cilantro, olives, and capers last.
- Drain excess marinade off fish, and pour on sauce. Cover and refrigerate for 3 hours before serving.
- Serve on Bibb lettuce, baby butter lettuce, or endive.
  Serves 10.

Try using scallops for a different base.

Mushrooms in Sour Cream with Watercress

¼ pound butter
1 small clove garlic, minced
4 cups fresh mushrooms, sliced
2 bunches fresh watercress,
  chop the tops only
1 tablespoons lemon juice,
  freshly squeezed

1 cup sour cream
½ teaspoon dry sherry
3 pieces thin sliced bread,
  toasted
extra watercress for garnish

- Melt butter in saucepan and add garlic and sliced mushrooms. Simmer for 15 minutes.
- Add watercress and lemon juice. Simmer another 20 minutes.
- Slowly add sour cream and allow it to heat for a few minutes.
- Add sherry and carefully mix.
- Place toast on plate and spoon mixture over it. Garnish with extra watercress.
  Serves 6.

Paloma Plantation Pecans

Great with coffee or as an appetizer.

2 cups sugar
1 tablespoon cinnamon,
  heaping
1 pinch salt

½ cup milk
1 teaspoon vanilla
5 cups pecan halves

- Combine sugar, cinnamon, salt, and milk in large teflon skillet.
- Cook over medium heat to the soft boil stage, stirring constantly.
- Remove from heat and add 1 teaspoon vanilla and 5 cups pecan halves.
- Stir to coat pecans.
- Pour onto wax paper and cool for 10 minutes. Break apart.
  Serves 10.

Green Pepper Jelly

4½ cups sugar
1½ cups white vinegar
1½ cups red pepper, minced
1 cup green pepper, minced

2 small dried chili peppers,
    seeded and crumbled
¾ teaspoon salt
1 bottle liquid pectin (6 ounces)

Serve with cream cheese and crackers as an appetizer, or as a condiment with meats.

- In a large sauce pan combine the sugar, vinegar, peppers, and salt.
- Bring to a boil, stirring until the sugar is dissolved.
- Stir in the liquid pectin and cook over medium-high heat until candy thermometer reaches 222°F.
- Seal in hot, sterilized jars. Process 10 minutes.
Makes 5 cups.

Green Indian Relish

10 green tomatoes
12 green peppers
6 red peppers
4 cups cabbage, shredded
½ cup salt
1 tablespoon celery seed

6 cups sugar
2 tablespoons mustard seed
1½ teaspoons tumeric
4 cups cider vinegar
2 cups water

Delicious on hamburgers and meats. It also makes a terrific gift.

- Coarsely grind the vegetables, using the metal blade of a food processor. Sprinkle with salt. Let sit overnight.
- Rinse mixture well and drain. Place in a large sauce pan and add remaining ingredients.
- Heat to boiling and simmer for 3 minutes. Seal in hot, sterilized jars. Process for 10 minutes.
Makes 20 cups.

Salsa Fresca

6 large tomatoes, chopped
4 Anaheim chilies, chopped
6 cloves garlic, minced
6 green onions, chopped
½ cup cilantro, chopped
1 cup dried chopped onions

1 tablespoon Louisiana hot
    sauce
1½ teaspoons salt
1 teaspoon ground mixed
    pepper
1 teaspoon garlic pepper
juice of one fresh lime

- Mix all ingredients together. Add more hot sauce or salt to taste.
- Serve with chips, fajitas or fish.
Makes 6 cups.

Soups

Southwestern Soup

Soup freezes well, and can be made ahead.

4 tablespoons butter
1 large onion, chopped
1⅓ cup raw white rice
3 quarts chicken broth
1 teaspoon cumin powder
2 cans (15.5 ounces) garbanzo
   beans, undrained
2 cans (14.5 ounces) gold or
   white hominy, undrained

2 cups diced cooked chicken or
   turkey
2 cans (4 ounces) diced green
   chilies
salt and pepper to taste
lime wedges
Monterey Jack cheese, grated
flour tortillas

- Sauté butter and onion for 5 minutes. Add rice and sauté until rice is opaque.
- Put rice mixture into large soup pot. Add broth, cumin, garbanzo beans, hominy, chicken or turkey, and diced green chilies.
- Cook 20 minutes.
- Season to taste. Garnish with chopped red peppers if desired.
- Serve with lime wedges and grated cheese. Warm tortillas go great with the soup.
Serves 12-16.

Squash Bisque

3 tablespoons butter
1 cup onion, minced
¼ cup carrot, minced
2 medium potatoes
2 acorn squashes

4 cups chicken stock or broth
½ cup half and half
½ cup milk
white pepper

- Add onions and carrots to melted butter in saucepan. Sprinkle with salt and white pepper. Cover with waxed paper and lid. Simmer for 10 minutes or until tender.
- Peel and cube potatoes and squashes.
- Add to onions and carrots. Add chicken stock and simmer covered over low heat for 25 minutes or until tender.
- Puree mixture. Return to pan and add cream and milk. Reheat through. Salt and pepper to taste.
Serves 8.

Green Chili Soup

1 onion, chopped
6 tablespoons unsalted butter
12 ounces green chilies,
   chopped
56 ounces plum tomatoes,
   drained
12 ounces cream cheese

29 ounces chicken broth
3 cups half and half or 2 cups
   milk
2 tablespoons plus 2 teaspoons
   lemon juice
cayenne

- Sauté onions in butter until soft.
- Add chilies and tomatoes. Cook 8-10 minutes until the liquid is gone.
- Stir in cream cheese until melted, but DO NOT BOIL.
- Stir in remaining ingredients and sprinkle each serving with a dash of cayenne.
- Serve warm or at room temperature.
  Serves 12-16.

Tortilla Soup

1 onion, chopped
1 can (4 ounces) chopped
   green chilies
1 garlic clove, minced
2 tablespoons oil
1 can (10¾ ounces) chicken
   broth
1 can (10¾ ounces) beef broth
1½ cups tomato juice
1½ cups water

1 large tomato, chopped
1 teaspoon cumin
2 tablespoons chili powder
1 teaspoon salt
1 cup fresh corn, optional
chicken pieces, optional
¼ cup grated cheese, Monterey
   Jack or Cheddar
4-6 corn tortillas

Makes a wonderful, colorful presentation.

- Sauté onion, green chilies and garlic in oil.
- Add remaining ingredients except cheese and tortillas. Bring to a boil.
- Simmer one hour. May be frozen at this point.
- 10 minutes before serving cut the tortillas into 1" strips. Fry them in a small amount of hot oil. Drain on paper towels.
- Add ¼ cup grated cheese and tortilla strips.
- Serve in bowls with a dollop of sour cream, extra cheese, and avocado.
  Serves 6.

Mexican Corn Chowder

2 tablespoons butter
1 large onion, chopped
2-3 garlic cloves, minced
2 tablespoons flour
2 packages (12 ounces) frozen
  whole kernel corn
1⅓ cups chicken stock
¼ cup fresh parsley, chopped

2 cups 2% milk
1 teaspoon salt
½ teaspoon freshly ground
  pepper
¼ teaspoon dried oregano
1 can (4 ounces) diced green
  chilies

Condiments:

1-2 cups Cheddar or Jack
  cheese, shredded
1 cup tomatoes, peeled, seeded,
  and diced
1 avocado, diced

1 chicken breast, cooked and
  julienned
6 slices bacon, fried crisp,
  drained, and crumbled
Tortilla strips

- Sauté onions and garlic in melted butter until the onions are soft, about 3-5 minutes.
- Blend in the flour. Cook until bubbly. Remove from heat.
- Blend in half of the corn, the chicken stock, and parsley.
- Pour mixture into a blender or food processor. Process until just blended. The mixture should not be smooth.
- Return mixture to the pan and reheat.
- Add the other half of the corn, the chicken stock, and parsley.
- Serve with condiments.
  Serves 4-6.

Chilled Shrimp Consommé

Can also serve molded and turned onto a leaf of lettuce for a salad.

1 can (11 ounces) consommé
  Madrilene
1 can (10¾ ounces) consommé
1 cup celery, chopped
½ cup scallions, chopped

2 tablespoons lemon juice
½ teaspoon curry powder
Tabasco to taste
1 cup Bay shrimp
Sour cream

- Combine all ingredients except sour cream in a bowl.
- Refrigerate at least 4 hours, or overnight.
- Serve cold with dollop of sour cream.
  Serves 4-6.

Chilled Cucumber-Tomato Soup

2 cans (10 ounces) tomato soup
2 soup cans of water
2 large cucumbers, peeled,
  halved, seeded, and shredded
½ cup green onion, chopped

2 teaspoons Worcestershire
  sauce
¼ teaspoon pepper
1 cup half and half
4 teaspoons fresh lemon juice

A fast and delicious summer soup.

- Pour the cans of tomato soup into a large bowl. Using a whisk add the water a little at a time, stirring constantly to avoid lumps.
- Add the cucumber, green onion, Worcestershire, and pepper. Stir to mix.
- Cover and chill overnight.
- Just before serving add the half and half and lemon juice. Blend.
  Serves 8.

Carrot and Tarragon Soup

2 tablespoons butter or
  margarine
2 medium onions, chopped
2 cloves garlic, minced
1½ pounds carrots, peeled and
  thinly sliced
1½ quarts chicken broth or 6
  cups water with 6 bouillon
  cubes

½ teaspoon dry tarragon
  leaves
½ teaspoon salt
¼ teaspoon pepper
½ cup orange juice
finely chopped parsley

- In a 5-6 quart kettle, sauté onion and garlic in butter for 5 minutes.
- Add carrots, chicken broth, tarragon, salt, and pepper. Bring to a boil.
- Cover kettle, reduce heat, and simmer until carrots are very tender, about 45 minutes.
- Set aside 1 cup of cooked carrot slices.
- Blend soup in blender until smooth.
- Return to kettle, add carrot slices and orange juice. Reheat.
- Garnish with parsley.
  Serves 6-8.

Pumpkin Shallot Soup

Can also use canned pumpkin, or butter nut squash as a substitute.

16 shallots
1 tablespoon olive oil
2 yellow onions, chopped
1 bunch leeks, cut in ⅛" rounds
3 cloves garlic, minced
½ teaspoon cumin
½ teaspoon oregano
½ teaspoon chili powder
½ teaspoon cayenne
½ bunch cilantro

¼ cup flour
4 cups beef broth
1 pound diced pumpkin
2 tablespoons tomato paste
1 large flour tortilla, cut in thin 1" pieces
1 tablespoon butter
crème fraîche (8 ounces sour cream and ½ pint whipping cream)

- Preheat oven to 375°.
- Toss shallots in oil, and arrange them on a cookie sheet. Bake until golden brown, turning occasionally, for 30 minutes.
- Sauté onions, leeks, and garlic. Add cumin, oregano, chili powder, cayenne, and chopped cilantro.
- Add ¼ cup flour. Cook for 10 minutes.
- Add 4 cups broth to blend with onion and flour mixture.
- Bring to a boil. Add pumpkin pieces and tomato paste. Simmer until pumpkin is cooked, about 20 minutes.
- Blend half of the soup mixture and all the pumpkin pieces in a Cuisinart.
- Return mixture to remaining soup. Add caramelized shallots 5 minutes before serving.
- In frying pan, melt 1 tablespoon butter and brown tortilla pieces until golden.
- Serve soup with hot tortilla pieces scattered on top and a dollop of crème fraîche.

Crème fraîche:
- Mix sour cream and whipping cream together. Allow mixture to sit for 24-36 hours at room temperature covered with a towel. Refrigerate. It will last for 1-2 weeks.

Serves 6-8.

Tomato Dill Soup

5 cups tomato juice
1 large Bermuda onion
3 stalks celery
¼ teaspoon basil

2 teaspoons whole dill seed
salt and pepper to taste
¾ cup sour cream
fresh dill garnish

- Cut vegetables into small pieces.
- Marinate in juice with seasonings overnight.
- Strain and stir in sour cream. French whisk can help get out any lumps.
- Serve very cold with sprig of fresh dill.
  Serves 6.

Great before a lamb dinner.

Zucchini Soup

1 cup onion, chopped
1 cup green pepper, chopped
3 tablespoons butter
6 cups zucchini, cut in chunks
1 clove garlic or 1 teaspoon
  garlic powder

1 teaspoon salt
¼ teaspoon pepper
2 tablespoons parsley
¼ teaspoon tarragon
2½ cups chicken broth
½ cup cream (optional)

- Sauté onion and green pepper in butter.
- Add zucchini chunks. Simmer 10 minutes.
- Add spices.
- Put in blender and blend until smooth.
- Add to chicken broth.
- Add cream if you want a creamier, richer soup.
- Serve hot or cold.
  Serves 8.

Great way to use those big zucchini from the garden.

Vegetable Cheese Chowder

Reduce the amount of corn-starch for a thinner soup.

3 chicken bouillon cubes
3 cups hot water
1 cup potatoes, chopped
½ cup carrots, chopped
½ cup celery, chopped
½ cup onion, chopped
½ cup green pepper, chopped

2 cups milk
¼ cup cornstarch
½ cup margarine
3 cups American or mild
  Cheddar cheese, shredded
dash pepper

- Put bouillon and water into soup pot. Bring to a boil.
- Add vegetables. Simmer 45 minutes.
- Combine the cornstarch and milk in a small bowl.
- Carefully stir the cornstarch mixture into the soup.
- May be made ahead and refrigerated at this point. Reheat just before serving.
- Add the margarine, cheese and pepper. Heat until the cheese melts.
  Serves 6.

Garbanzo Soup

Easy to cook in a crockpot, and is low in calories!

1 teaspoon virgin olive oil
1 small onion, chopped
1 garlic clove, minced
1 celery stalk, sliced
1 cup canned Italian Plum
  tomatoes, with liquid
1 carrot, sliced
½ small red pepper, diced

½ teaspoon dried basil leaf or
  1½ teaspoon fresh
1 cup canned chickpeas
  (garbanzos), drained and
  rinsed
4 cups chicken broth
salt and pepper to taste

- Sauté onion, garlic and celery for 5 minutes in heated oil. Add remaining ingredients.
- Bring to a boil, reduce heat and simmer covered for 20 minutes.
  Serves 6.

Harvest Soup

6 slices bacon
2 tablespoons butter
¾ cup onion, chopped
¾ cup celery, chopped
4 cups chicken stock or broth
2 cups potatoes with skins,
  diced

6 cups fresh corn or 3 frozen
  packages (10 ounces),
  thawed
1 can (4 ounces) diced green
  chilies
1 cup heavy cream
salt and pepper to taste

- Fry bacon until crisp. Remove.
- Add butter to bacon drippings. Sauté onion and celery until tender.
- Simmer potatoes in chicken broth until tender.
- Puree 4 cups (2 packages) of corn in blender adding a few table-spoons of hot broth while blending.
- Add pureed corn, remaining whole corn, vegetables, green chilies with liquid, and cream to soup pot. Season with salt and pepper.
- Just before serving, crumble bacon into soup reserving a small amount to crumble on top in bowls.
  Serves 6-8.

Lentil Soup

2 cups lentils, rinsed well
3 cups beef broth
5 ribs of celery, finely chopped
5 carrots, finely chopped
1½ cups canned tomatoes,
  drained and chopped
¼ cup olive oil
1 onion, finely chopped

½ cup fresh parsley, minced
¼ pound ham, diced
2 garlic cloves, minced
1½ teaspoons salt
½ teaspoon pepper
2 tablespoons lemon juice
½ cup Parmesan, grated

- In a large pot combine all ingredients EXCEPT the cheese. Add 7 cups of water.
- Boil and simmer, covered for 1½ hours. Skim off froth.
- Ladle into bowls and sprinkle with the Parmesan.
  Serves 8-10.

Hearty Vegetable Soup

1 pound ground chuck
½ teaspoon ground black
  pepper
1 teaspoon Worcestershire
½ tablespoon sugar
1 tablespoon basil
1 can (2½ pounds) tomatoes
1 can (8 ounces) tomato sauce

1½ cups potatoes, cubed
½ cup onion, chopped
1 cup celery, chopped
½ cup fresh parsley, chopped
2 cans beef bouillon
1 box (10 ounces) frozen mixed
  vegetables

- Brown the meat.
- Add remaining ingredients EXCEPT the frozen vegetables.
- Simmer one hour.
- Add frozen vegetables. Cook another hour. Skim fat off top, if
  necessary.
  Serves 8-10.

Wild Rice Soup

A very elegant soup.

6 tablespoons butter
1 tablespoon onion, minced
½ cup flour
3 cups chicken broth
2 cups cooked wild rice
⅓ cup ham, minced

½ cup carrots, finely grated
3 tablespoons slivered almonds,
  chopped
1 cup half and half
2 tablespoons dry sherry
minced parsley

- Sauté onion in butter until tender.
- Blend in flour and gradually add broth. Stir constantly until the
  mixture comes to a boil.
- Boil 1 minute. Stir in rice, ham, carrots, almonds, and salt.
- Simmer 5 minutes.
- Blend in half and half and sherry.
- Heat to serving temperature.
- Garnish with minced parsley.
  Serves 6-8.

Veal and Tortellini Soup

Soup base:

1 tablespoon olive oil
1 tablespoon butter
2 ribs celery, chopped
1 onion, chopped
1 can (49.5 ounces) chicken
   stock
8 tablespoons tomato paste
1 ham hock

½ cup canned kidney beans
1 cup fresh spinach, cut in
   pieces
½ cup small Parmesan
   tortellini, available prepared
   in markets
juice of half a lemon

Meatballs:

½ pound ground veal
1 egg, beaten
1 tablespoon Parmesan, grated

1 tablespoon flour
2 tablespoons parsley, chopped
salt and pepper to taste

Soup base:

- Soften onion and celery in butter and oil.
- Add a little stock and puree onion and celery in food processor.
- In a large saucepan, combine the rest of the stock and the tomato paste.
- Add the pureed mixture and ham hock. Simmer at least half an hour.

Meatballs:

- Mix all ingredients together in a bowl. Form into little balls.
- 20 minutes before serving, remove the ham hock from the pan. Add the beans, tortellini, and meat balls.
- Simmer for 15-20 minutes.
- Add spinach and lemon juice just before serving.
  Serves 4-6.

Beef Borscht

You won't believe how delicious this soup is with the culmination of these ingredients!

3 pounds stew beef, cubed
5 cans (10.5 ounces) beef
  bouillon
3-4 carrots, sliced ¼ -½"
2 celery ribs, sliced
1 medium onion, chopped
2 teaspoons salt
½ teaspoon pepper
½ teaspoon dill weed

2 bay leaves
2 teaspoons sugar
½ cup dill pickle juice
1 can (6 ounces) tomato paste
2 tablespoons red wine vinegar
1 can (16 ounces) julienne
  beets, undrained
4 cups red cabbage, shredded
1 cup sour cream

- In a Dutch oven or large roaster pan, combine the following: beef, bouillon, carrots, celery, onion, and seasonings. Cover and bake at 300° for about 3-4 hours or until meat is tender.
- Add cabbage and cook covered for another ½ hour.
- Discard bay leaves.
- Add beets and vinegar.
- Stir in ⅓ cup sour cream prior to finishing.
- Top each serving bowl with a dollop of remaining sour cream. **Serves 6-8.**

Italian Sausage Soup

1½ pounds Italian sausage, cut
  in ½" lengths
2 cloves garlic, minced
2 large onions, chopped
1 can (28 ounces) Italian
  tomatoes
3 cans (14 ounces) beef broth
1½ cups dry red wine

½ teaspoon basil leaves,
  crumbled
3 tablespoons parsley, chopped
1 green pepper, chopped
2 medium zucchini, sliced ¼"
  thick
3 cups uncooked noodles
Parmesan cheese, grated

- Cook sausage in 5 quart Dutch oven over medium heat until lightly browned. Pour off fat.
- Add garlic and onions. Cook, stirring until limp.
- Stir in tomatoes, breaking them up with a spoon.
- Add broth, wine, and basil. Simmer uncovered for 30 minutes.
- Add parsley, pepper, zucchini, and noodles. Simmer covered for 25 minutes or until noodles are tender.
- Sprinkle individual servings with grated Parmesan cheese. **Serves 6.**

Calcutta Mulligatawny Soup

3½ pounds broiler chicken, cut
  up
¼ cup unsifted flour
¼ cup butter or margarine
1 cup onion, chopped
1 cup carrot, chopped
1 cup celery, chopped
1 cup pared tart apple,
  chopped

3 teaspoons curry powder
2 teaspoons salt
½ teaspoon mace
¼ teaspoon pepper
¼ teaspoon chili powder
½ cup flaked coconut
5 cups cold water or chicken
  stock

*This is also great
served on top of
rice and gar-
nished with
parsley.*

- Dredge chicken pieces in flour. Sauté in butter until well browned. Push to one side.
- Add onion, carrot, celery, apple, and remaining flour. Cook, stirring for 5 minutes.
- Add remaining ingredients plus 5 cups cold water or chicken stock. Mix well and bring to a boil.
- Reduce heat and simmer covered for 1 hour. Remove chicken.
- Simmer soup covered for another hour, stirring frequently.
- Skim fat from top.
- Remove chicken from bones.
- Puree the soup. Return the chicken. Reheat.
  Serves 4-6.

Fisherman's Chowder

5 strips bacon, chopped
2 large onions, chopped
1 can (14 ounces) chicken
  broth
2 cups potatoes, diced small
1 pound fish, bite size pieces
2 cups half and half, scalded

fresh ground black pepper
3 tablespoons margarine or
  butter
2 tablespoons fresh parsley
1 bay leaf
dash thyme

*Best if made in
advance and
reheated.
Use halibut, cod,
flounder, or sole.*

- Cook the bacon until crisp.
- Add the onion. Cook until tender.
- Add broth and potatoes. Cook gently for 10 minutes.
- Add fish. Simmer for 5 minutes.
- Add remaining ingredients and heat briefly, being careful not to over cook.
  Serves 4.

Christmas Eve Oyster Soup

2 cans (8 ounces) whole
  oysters
1 bottle (8 ounces) clam juice
4 stalks celery, thinly sliced
4 scallions, thinly sliced

4 tablespoons unsalted butter
1 pint heavy whipping cream
1 teaspoon thyme
3 medium red skinned potatoes
salt and pepper to taste

- Microwave potatoes whole for 2-3 minutes. Chop.
- Sauté celery and scallions in butter.
- Add remaining ingredients and simmer for 1 hour.
  Serves 4.

Chili Companero

*This chili also
freezes very well.*

*You may also
leave the chili
peppers whole
and remove them
when you serve.*

1½ pounds lean ground beef or
  sirloin
1 small onion, minced
salt, pepper and garlic salt to
  taste
2 cans (28 ounces) whole
  tomatoes

1 package of French's Chili-O's
1 cup water
1 jigger of Cuervo Gold tequila
3 yellow chili peppers, minced
1 can (23 ounces) chili beans

- Sauté meat with onion, salt, pepper, and garlic salt. Drain.
- Mix remaining ingredients in an 8 quart stock pot. Add meat. Cook
  at a high temperature, stirring occasionally, until the chili boils.
- Reduce temperature and simmer for 1½ hours.
- Serve with oyster crackers and top with cheddar cheese.
  Serves 6-8.

Chunky Chili

4 tablespoons vegetable oil
2 large onions, chopped
4 cloves garlic, minced
4 pounds stew beef, cubed
3 pounds bulk spicy pork
  sausage
2 cans (28 ounces) whole
  tomatoes
1 can (15 ounces) tomato
  sauce
6 tablespoons chili powder
3 tablespoons cumin

2 tablespoons oregano
2 cans (1 pound) baked beans,
  undrained
2 teaspoons salt
2 tablespoons sugar
1 tablespoon unsweetened
  cocoa powder
2 cans (15 ounces) kidney
  beans
1 can (15 ounces) pinto beans
1 can (4 ounces) diced green
  chilies

A great dish to take on ski trips.

- Sauté onion and garlic until soft in large dutch oven.
- Add beef and sausage. Cook until brown. Pour off fat.
- Add liquid from tomatoes. Chop the tomatoes and add to meat. Add tomato sauce, chili powder, cumin, oregano, baked beans, salt, sugar, and cocoa powder.
- Simmer, partially covered for 2 hours, stirring often.
- Stir in kidney beans and pinto beans. Cook 1½ hours longer, until tender.
- At this point you can refrigerate a day ahead or freeze.
- To serve, reheat slowly until bubbly.
- Serve with grated cheese, sour cream, small corn chips, or sliced black olives.
Serves 16.

Salads

Hearts of Palm with Tangy Lemon Dressing

*A salad men
really love.*

2-3 heads Boston lettuce, torn
  in bite-size pieces
5 green onions, sliced (no tops)

1 can (14 ounces) Hearts of
  Palm, drained and sliced
  horizontally

Lemon Cream Dressing:
2 cloves garlic, crushed
2 teaspoons sugar
1 grated whole lemon rind
1 teaspoon seasoned salt

½ teaspoon cracked pepper
¼ teaspoon paprika
6 tablespoons fresh lemon juice
6 tablespoons sour cream

Dressing:
- Blend all ingredients until smooth. Shake before using.
- Toss lettuce, onions, and hearts of palm in dressing. Greens should be nicely coated. You may not use all of the dressing.
Serves 8.

Designer Salad

*Spectacular
presentation for a
dinner party.*

¾ pound Roquefort cheese
¾ cup unsalted butter
3-4 heads Bibb lettuce

1 recipe Vinaigrette Dressing
2 tablespoons fresh parsley,
  chopped

Vinaigrette Dressing:
2 tablespoons vinegar (red,
  white, tarragon or cider)
½ cup oil (vegetable, olive, or
  peanut)

1 teaspoon salt
½ teaspoon freshly cracked
  black pepper

- Beat cheese and butter together until creamy. Place a mound of cheese into center of each salad plate.
- Poke the stems of 6-7 lettuce leaves into each mound. It should look like a small head of lettuce.
- Spoon 2 tablespoons vinaigrette over each salad. Sprinkle with parsley.
Vinaigrette:
- Place all ingredients in jar and shake.
Serves 6-8.

Green Salad with Raspberry Vinaigrette

1 head Romaine or green leaf
lettuce
1 small jicama, peeled and
julienned

2 cans (10.5 ounces) mandarin
oranges, drained
1 avocado, sliced
⅔ cup toasted, slivered
almonds

Raspberry Vinaigrette:

1 can (12 ounces)
raspberry/cranberry frozen
concentrate juice
1 jar (16 ounces) seedless
raspberry jam
2 cups red wine vinegar

4 cups safflower oil
2 teaspoons fresh garlic,
minced
1 teaspoon white pepper
½ teaspoon salt

Vinaigrette makes a beautiful gift anytime of the year.

Vinaigrette:
- Put all ingredients EXCEPT vinegar and oil in food processor or large blender. Process until smooth.
- Add vinegar. Process 1-2 minutes.
- Slowly drizzle the oil in as the processor is running. (This keeps the dressing from separating.)

Salad:
- Arrange the ingredients in bowl in order listed. Add vinaigrette to taste.
  Makes 2 quarts of dressing.
  Salad serves 6-8.

Linda Bosse's fabulous recipe that
she served at Slight Indulgence.

Chilled Herbed Tomatoes

8 ripe tomatoes
1¼ teaspoon salt
¼ teaspoon pepper
¾ teaspoon thyme

⅓ cup fresh parsley, minced
½ cup green onions, chopped
¾ cup salad oil
⅓ cup tarragon vinegar

Scrumptious!

- Peel and slice tomatoes. Place on serving platter.
- Mix remaining ingredients. Pour over tomatoes.
- Chill 4 hours or overnight. Keeps well for a couple of days.
  Serves 12-16.

Marinated Mushroom and Cauliflower Salad

1 pound fresh mushrooms, sliced
1 cup salad oil
½ cup red wine vinegar
2 tablespoons onion, finely minced
1½ teaspoons salt
1 teaspoon sugar

½ teaspoon ground black pepper
¼ teaspoon dry mustard
½ medium sized cauliflower, cut in flowerettes and sliced thinly
1 cup celery, sliced
1 green pepper, cut in strips
8 cherry tomatoes, halved

- Rinse, pat dry and thinly slice mushrooms. Set aside.
- In a large bowl combine oil, vinegar, onion, salt, sugar, pepper, and mustard.
- Add mushrooms and toss to coat.
- Add cauliflower, pepper, and celery. Let marinate for 1 hour.
- Top with tomatoes right before serving.
  Serves 8.

Caesar Salad

The dressing may be made the night before.

1 clove garlic, pressed
1-2 ounces anchovy paste
½ teaspoon ground pepper
¼ cup olive oil
¼ cup vegetable oil
1 tablespoon Dijon mustard
3 tablespoons lemon juice

1 egg
1 head Romaine lettuce, rinsed and dried
¼ cup fresh Parmesan cheese, shredded
1 cup croutons

- Mix together garlic, anchovy paste, and pepper in a bowl. Add mustard, lemon juice, and egg.
- Mix oils together. Slowly add to above, beating continuously with a wire whisk.
- Pour dressing over lettuce. Sprinkle with Parmesan cheese and croutons. Toss and serve immediately.
  Serves 4-6.

Oriental Slaw

½ head green cabbage,
  shredded coarsely
3 green onions, sliced
3 tablespoons slivered
  almonds, toasted
3 tablespoons sesame seeds,
  toasted

4 ounces water chestnuts,
  sliced
1 package (3 ounces) chicken
  flavor Oriental noodle soup
  (Top Ramen)

Add warm grilled chicken breasts to make this a summer entree salad for a luncheon.

Dressing:
5½ tablespoons rice wine
  vinegar
1 cup vegetable oil

¼ teaspoon garlic powder
1 teaspoon sugar
ground pepper to taste

- Toss first five ingredients together in a serving bowl. Sprinkle seasoning packet from soup mix over mixture.
- Break noodles apart and mix into cabbage mixture.
- Toss with enough dressing to moisten and flavor (about ⅓ -½ for 4 servings). Serve immediately.

Dressing:
- Combine all ingredients and mix well.
  Serves 4.

Stoplight Salad

1 package (10 ounces) frozen
  peas, thawed
1 package (10 ounces) frozen
  corn, thawed
1 jar (2 ounces) chopped
  pimentos

3 hard-boiled eggs, chopped
1 medium onion, diced
½ cup mayonnaise
Lawry's Seasoning Salt

- Mix together corn and peas. Add remaining vegetables and eggs.
- Sprinkle generously with seasoned salt.
- Add enough mayonnaise to coat. Refrigerate and serve in a lettuce lined bowl. Sprinkle with seasoned salt just before serving.
  Serves 6.

Southwest Black Bean Salad

Phoenix favorite.

1½ cups cooked black beans
1 head Romaine lettuce
1 head red leaf lettuce
1 bunch green onions, chopped
1 cucumber, sliced
2 tomatoes, chopped
2 avocados, chopped
2 cups blue corn chips, broken
1 cup Cheddar cheese, grated

1 cup pepper Jack cheese,
  grated
1 teaspoon chili powder
1 teaspoon cumin
1 teaspoon cayenne red pepper
1 teaspoon garlic powder
¾ cup cooked wild rice
French dressing

- Mix chili powder, cumin, cayenne, and garlic powder together with wild rice.
- Combine all ingredients together. Add French dressing to coat. **Serves 10.**

Colorful Black Bean Salad

2 cans (15 ounces) black
  beans, drained and rinsed
1 can (11 ounces) crisp niblet
  corn, drained
1 medium red bell pepper,
  chopped

1 small bunch green onions,
  chopped
1 small red onion, chopped
3 cloves garlic, minced
2 teaspoons fresh basil,
  chopped
green peppers or tomatoes

Dressing:
1½ teaspoons salt
1 teaspoon sugar
1 teaspoon mixed pepper

⅓ cup red wine vinegar
¼ cup light olive oil

- Combine all of the salad ingredients together.
- Mix dressing ingredients together. Pour over bean mixture
- Serve in half green pepper or half tomato shells. **Serves 10-12.**

Oaxacan Fruit Salad

½ pineapple, peeled, cored,
   and cut into wedges
1 papaya, seeded and cut into
   squares
2 cups watermelon balls
Honey Poppy Seed Dressing

2 Haas avocados, cut into thin,
   long strips
1 pomegranate
1 head red leaf lettuce, rinsed
   and blotted dry

Honey Poppy Seed Dressing:

¾ cup fragrant blossom honey
1 teaspoon salt
1 teaspoon dry mustard
⅓ cup white wine vinegar

1½ tablespoons onion, chopped
1½ tablespoons poppy seeds
1 cup oil, soy or peanut

Dressing:
• Place all the ingredients in a blender jar or food processor and
  process until well blended. Keep at room temperature until ready to
  use.

Salad:
• Cut all fruit as directed. Combine all but the avocado and pome-
  granate.
• Add the dressing to fruit and gently toss.
• Arrange on lettuce leaves in a bowl. Spoon the salad onto the leaves
  and garnish with avocado. Spoon remaining dressing from bowl
  over the top.
• Peel the pomegranate. Carefully pick out the red seeds and sprinkle
  over the salad.
  Serves 6.

Joanne Menapace, Chef
Cathy's Rum Cake Caterers

Apple Walnut Salad with Feta Cheese

1 large head Bibb lettuce, torn
   into bite size pieces
1 large red Delicious apple,
   diced

1 package (2 ounces) walnuts,
   diced
4 ounces Feta cheese,
   crumbled
1 teaspoon lemon juice

• Sprinkle diced apple with lemon juice.
• Combine all ingredients and toss with Raspberry Vinaigrette,
  (recipe on page 49).
  Serves 4.

Tangy Horseradish Spinach Salad

2 bunches spinach, cleaned
   and torn into bite size pieces

1 cup dry cottage cheese
1 cup pecans, chopped

Dressing:
1 cup sour cream
3 tablespoons vinegar

2 tablespoons horseradish,
   creme style
½ teaspoon dry mustard

- Toss salad ingredients together.
- Combine dressing ingredients and let sit. Add to spinach right before serving.
  Serves 6-8.

Fruit and Spinach Salad

8 slices bacon
½ cup almonds, sliced
10 cups spinach, rinsed and
   torn into pieces
1 small Pippin apple, cored
   and chopped

1 small red delicious apple,
   cored and chopped
1 small pear, cored and
   chopped
4 green onions, sliced
1 teaspoon honey

Dressing:
¼ cup vegetable oil
3 tablespoons raspberry
   vinegar

½ teaspoon mustard
salt and pepper to taste

- Cook bacon in a skillet until crisp. Drain and crumble.
- In bacon grease, sauté almonds until brown.
- Combine spinach, bacon, almonds, fruit, and onions. Coat with honey.
- Mix dressing ingredients together and refrigerate.
- Toss salad with dressing when ready to serve.
  Serves 8.

Spinach Rice Salad

1 cup rice
½ cup bottled Italian dressing
1 tablespoon soy sauce
½ teaspoon sugar

2 cups fresh spinach, cut into
* thin strips*
½ cup celery, sliced
½ cup green onion, sliced
⅓ cup crumbled crisp bacon

- Cook rice according to directions. Transfer rice to bowl and cool slightly.
- Combine dressing, soy sauce and sugar. Stir mixture into warm rice.
- Cover and chill. Fold in remaining ingredients before serving.
  Serves 6-8.

Spinach Chutney Salad

1 pound fresh spinach, washed
* and trimmed*
¾ cup fresh bean sprouts
6 slices bacon, cooked and
* crumbled*
¾ cup mushrooms, sliced

1 cup water chestnut slices
½ cup Swiss or Gruyère
* cheese, shredded*
¼ cup red onion, sliced and
* pulled in circles*

Dressing:
¼ cup wine vinegar
3 tablespoons Major Gray's
* Chutney*
1 clove garlic

2 tablespoons Dijon mustard
1 teaspoon sugar
½ cup vegetable oil
salt and pepper to taste

Dressing:
- Process all ingredients EXCEPT oil in blender until smooth. Add oil slowly until thick.
- Refrigerate.
- Toss salad ingredients and add dressing to taste.
  Serves 4-6.

Curried Spinach Salad

8 cups fresh spinach, torn
1½ cups apple, chopped with
    skin on
½-¾ cup golden raisins

12 fresh mushrooms, sliced
½ cup peanuts, chopped
2-3 tablespoons green onion,
    chopped

Dressing:
¼ cup red wine vinegar
½ cup olive oil
2 tablespoons chutney,
    chopped

½ teaspoon sugar
½ teaspoon salt
1½ teaspoons curry powder
1 teaspoon dry mustard

- Combine all salad ingredients in a bowl or shallow platter.
- Combine dressing ingredients in a jar and shake. Chill.
- Toss salad with dressing when ready to serve.
  Serves 6-8.

Broccoli Delight

1 pound fresh broccoli
1 pound bacon, cooked and
    crumbled
1 small red onion, chopped
½ cup raisins

¾ cup currants and peanuts,
    crushed
1 cup mayonnaise
½ cup sugar
2 teaspoons vinegar

- Cut broccoli into bite-size pieces.
- Trim the stems by cutting off the outside darker green skin. Slice diagonally into ¼" circles.
- Place in small bowl. Add the bacon, onion, raisins, currents, and nuts.
- In a small bowl whisk together the mayonnaise, sugar, and vinegar.
- Toss dressing with salad about an hour or two before serving.
  Serves 6-8.

Special thanks to Arcadia Farms
for sharing this recipe with us.

Summer Pasta Salad

Dressing:

⅔ cup red wine vinegar
¾ cup parsley, chopped
6-8 teaspoons Dijon mustard
1 clove garlic

2 cups light olive oil or canola
  oil
salt and pepper to taste
1-1½ cups fresh basil leaves

Salad:

8-10 ounces tortellini or
  swirled pasta
1 red pepper, diced
½ cup red onion, diced
1 green pepper, diced
1 small jicama, diced

2 cups cooked chicken, ham, or
  beef, diced
2 cups salami, diced
2 cups Pine nuts
2 cups fresh Parmesan cheese,
  grated

Dressing:
- Place garlic and basil in a processor. Process.
- Add remaining ingredients and process until well incorporated.

Salad:
- Cook and drain pasta. Toss with a little light oil.
- Add the remaining ingredients to the pasta.
- Toss with the dressing.
- Add extra fresh basil and cheese just before serving and toss again
  to mix ingredients.
- **Serves 8-10.**

A special thank you to Barbara Colleary
of Culinary Creations for sharing this recipe
with the Junior League of Phoenix.

Shrimp Ceviche

A spicy, local recipe.
If you have problems finding the peppers, use canned green chilies.

2 packages (8 ounces) cooked frozen baby shrimp, thawed
10 green onions, chopped
10 hot chili peppers, split and seeded (1" pale green pickled in jar)

1 cup lemon or lime juice
3½ tablespoons ketchup
2 tomatoes, chopped
cilantro, chopped

- Mix shrimp, onion, and pepper. Cover with lemon or lime juice. Add ketchup.
- Marinate for 12 hours or longer.
- Two hours before serving remove peppers and add tomatoes.
- Serve on lettuce cup or in a bowl. Top with cilantro.
  Serves 8.

Spicy Oriental Chicken Salad

This is also great as an appetizer with double the amount of red pepper flakes, and served on the tip of endive lettuce leaves.

4 tablespoons ginger root, coarsely chopped
4 chicken breast halves
4 tablespoons soy sauce
2 tablespoons sherry
4 teaspoons sesame oil
¼ teaspoon red pepper flakes

2 teaspoons sugar
4 tablespoons scallions, chopped
4 tablespoons cilantro, chopped
2 cups water chestnuts, chopped
Bibb lettuce

- In a large sauce pan with a tight fitting lid, place 2 cups water and ginger root. Bring to a boil, then simmer 15 minutes. Cool and chop.
- Place chicken, breasts side down, in boiling liquid. Cover and reduce heat to low. Poach 15 minutes or until done. Remove and cool.
- In a large bowl, combine soy sauce, sherry, sesame oil, red pepper flakes, sugar, scallions, cilantro, and water chestnuts. Mix well.
- Add 1 teaspoon chopped ginger to soy mixture.
- Finely shred chicken meat from breasts and add to marinade. Chill for 30 minutes.
- Serve on a bed of Bibb lettuce.
  Serves 4-6.

Pinon Chicken Salad

¼ cup Pine nuts
1 pound spinach
2 tablespoons unsalted butter,
  melted
3 medium shallots, finely
  chopped
½ cup ricotta cheese
1 egg yolk

⅛ teaspoon black pepper
½ teaspoon seasoning salt
1 slice prosciutto, ⅛" thick
2 chicken breast halves, boned
3 tablespoons unsalted butter,
  melted
3 tablespoons lemon juice
4 tablespoons mayonnaise

- Toast Pine nuts in oven for 5 minutes at 350°. Set aside.
- Steam spinach and finely chop.
- Sauté shallots in butter.
- Combine above ingredients with salt, pepper, egg yolk, and cheese.
- Place prosciutto on chicken. Spread with filling and roll small end up. Place seam side down on greased casserole dish.
- Mix butter and lemon juice. Spoon over chicken. Bake 20-25 minutes at 375°. Baste with pan juice.
- Chill. Slice and serve on lettuce leaves. Mix a little lemon juice with mayonnaise to place on top of each piece.
  Serves 4-6.

Santa Fe Turkey and Rice Salad

An exciting main dish salad.

Salad:
2 cups long grain white rice
4 cups water
4 cups cubed turkey, cooked
2 large tomatoes, coarsely chopped

2 cups bell pepper, finely diced
2 cups corn, freshly cooked or thawed, if frozen
⅔ cup red onion, chopped

Dressing:
1 cup oil (olive or vegetable)
1 bunch cilantro, finely chopped
6 tablespoons white wine vinegar
2 tablespoons Dijon mustard

1 can (4 ounces) diced green chilies, drained
2½ teaspoons ground cumin
1 teaspoon salt
1 teaspoon pepper

Garnish:
red leaf lettuce

1 ripe avocado, peeled and sliced

- Bring water to boil. Add rice, cover and cook over low heat 20 minutes. Transfer to bowl and cool.
- Add turkey, tomatoes, bell pepper, corn, and onion. Toss.
- Whisk together all dressing ingredients. Pour over salad. Toss gently.
- Serve at room temperature or cover and refrigerate for 3 hours.
- Arrange lettuce leaves on platter. Mound salad in center. Garnish with avocado slices.
  Serves 8.

Cayenne Chicken Salad

*3 chicken breast halves, boned
   and skinned*
1 cup milk
4 tablespoons flour
½ teaspoon cayenne pepper
½ teaspoon paprika
½ teaspoon chili powder

¼ teaspoon pepper
Butter lettuce
1 can (16 ounces) corn, drained
Ranch style dressing (8 ounces)
¾ cup cashews or pecans
peanut oil

- Shake seasonings in a baggie. Dip chicken in milk and coat in baggie. Fry in small amount of peanut oil. Drain.
- Add chicken to lettuce, corn, and cashews. Toss with ranch dressing.
Serves 4.

Blue Cheese Dressing

*1 large garlic clove, finely
   chopped*
¼ teaspoon salt
1 tablespoon Dijon mustard
2 tablespoons lemon juice

2 tablespoons tarragon vinegar
⅓ cup olive oil
⅓ cup sour cream
¾ cup Blue cheese, crumbled

- Blend all ingredients EXCEPT Blue cheese in a blender or food processor.
- Fold in Blue cheese for a chunky texture, or process together for creamier texture.

Breads

Herb Bread

There is a wonderful aroma as this bread bakes.

1 loaf of unsliced butter crust
  bread
1½ sticks butter
¾ teaspoon marjoram
¾ teaspoon thyme

1 teaspoon powdered garlic
1 tablespoon Worchestershire
  sauce
¼ teaspoon Accent

- Cut all crust off the bread. Make one long cut lengthwise, not through the bottom. Make 5 cross-wise cuts evenly spaced, not through the bottom.
- Mix all spices with the butter.
- Spread butter mixture between each slice of bread, and over the outside of the loaf.
- Place loaf in a bread pan and bake at 350° for 25-30 minutes. **Serves 8-10.**

Spedini Alla Romana

Great with a green salad and wine for a late night gathering.

1 long loaf of Italian Bread
1 stick butter
¼ cup chopped onion
2-3 tablespoons Dijon mustard

1 tablespoon poppy seeds
½ pound sliced Swiss cheese
5 slices bacon, cut in half

- Trim most of the crust from the top and sides of bread. Slash almost to the bottom at one inch intervals.
- Sauté chopped onion in butter until wilted. Stir in mustard and poppy seeds.
- Spread between slashes of bread.
- Insert the slices of cheese between the slashes of bread.
- Arrange bacon over the top of the loaf.
- Bake at 350° for 30-40 minutes until bacon is crisp and cheese is melted. **Serves 4-6.**

Fresh Herb Butter

¼ cup green onion, chopped
½ pound butter, softened
3 tablespoons fresh basil, chopped

3 tablespoons fresh dill, minced
1 teaspoon dry mustard
¼ cup fresh parsley, minced

- Blend softened butter with the green onion, basil, dill, mustard, and parsley.
- Slice a loaf of French bread almost through, and spread the butter on both sides of the slices.
- Wrap in foil and bake in a 350° oven for 20-30 minutes.
- Keeps well in the refrigerator and can be made ahead by a couple of days.
  Serves 12.

Pretty served in a basket on a buffet table with the slices pulled apart.

Dilly Bread

3 cups flour
1 tablespoon sugar
2 teaspoons instant minced onion
2 teaspoons dried dill weed
¼ teaspoon soda

1 teaspoon salt
2 packages dry yeast
1 cup creamed cottage cheese
¾ cup water
1 egg

- Combine 1½ cups flour, sugar, onion, dill weed, soda, salt, and yeast in large mixing bowl.
- Combine cottage cheese and water in a small sauce pan. Heat to 110°. Do not boil.
- Add egg and warm liquid to flour. Beat 3 minutes.
- Add remaining flour by hand. Let rest 15 minutes.
- Turn into greased 1½ quart casserole or 9x5 loaf pan. Cover with a towel and let rise until doubled.
- Bake at 350° for 45-60 minutes. Cool before slicing.
  Serves 8-10.

Can add 2 table-spoons of butter to the cottage cheese and water if a richer flavor is desired.

Guilt-Free Carrot Bread

Low in sugar and fat!

1½ cups flour
1 cup carrots, shredded
1 teaspoon baking soda
1 teaspoon cinnamon
¼ teaspoon salt
½ cup sugar

⅓ cup oil
¼ cup apple juice
½ teaspoon vanilla
2 eggs, lightly beaten
½ cup raisins
¼ cup walnuts, chopped

- In a medium bowl, combine flour, carrots, raisins, nuts, baking soda, cinnamon, and salt. Set aside.
- In a large bowl, stir together sugar, oil, apple juice and vanilla. Add eggs and stir until blended. Add flour-carrot mixture and mix well.
- Spoon into 8½ x 4½ loaf pan. Bake 50-60 minutes at 350°. **Serves 6-8.**

Honey Wheat Rolls

2 cups warm water (100° F.)
⅓ cup honey
1 tablespoon olive oil
2 packages active dry yeast
1 teaspoon anise seed
1 tablespoon salt

3 cups whole wheat flour
3 cups unbleached flour
1 egg, beaten with 2
  tablespoons water
Sesame seeds

- Combine the water, honey, oil, yeast, anise seed, and salt in a large ceramic bowl. Allow the mixture to stand for 15 minutes to let the yeast grow and bubble.
- Add the flours to make a soft dough. Knead the dough for 5 minutes or until elastic.
- Place the dough into another slightly oiled bowl and place in a warm area until doubled in bulk, about 45 minutes. Loosely cover with a towel.
- Punch down the dough with a fist. Using small pieces of the dough slightly larger than a golf ball, make the rolls and place on a non-stick or slightly oiled baking pan.
- Brush the rolls with the beaten egg mixture, and sprinkle with sesame seeds.
- Place the rolls in a warm area and let rise until double in bulk.
- Bake in a preheated oven (350°) for about 20 minutes.
Makes 36 rolls.

Irresistible Cheese Bread

1¼ teaspoons active dry yeast
3 tablespoons butter
¾ cup milk
1 large egg, unbeaten
⅛ cup sugar
¾ teaspoon salt

2½ to 2¾ cups unbleached all
   purpose flour
½ pound Mozzarella cheese,
   cut into ¼" cubes
½ pound Muenster cheese, cut
   into ¼" cubes

*Almost a meal
within itself!*

- In a large bowl proof the yeast in ⅛ cup lukewarm water for 5 minutes, or until it is foamy.
- In a small saucepan melt the butter. Add the milk and heat to lukewarm.
- Stir the milk mixture into the yeast mixture. Add the unbeaten egg, sugar, and salt. Combine well.
- Stir in 2 cups of the flour. Add ½ cup of the remaining flour. Mix well.
- Add enough of the remaining ¼ cup of flour to form a soft, smooth dough.
- Knead 3 minutes and form into a ball. Put into a lightly buttered bowl, turning to coat with butter. Loosely cover with a towel. Let rise for 2 hours. Punch down, cover, and let rise again for 1 hour.
- Roll out ball into an oval (16x13). Sprinkle the cheese on the lengthwise half. Fold over and seal the edges well using brushed on beaten egg. Pinch edges together.
- Transfer to a baking sheet and pierce all over with a fork. Brush lightly with beaten egg. Bake at 400° for 20-25 minutes or until golden brown.
Serves 6-8.

Green Chile Cornbread

½ pound butter
1 cup sugar
4 eggs
1 can (4 ounces) chopped
   green chilies
1 can (16.5 ounces) cream
   style corn

½ cup grated Monterey Jack
   cheese
½ cup grated Cheddar cheese
¼ teaspoon salt
1 cup flour
1 cup yellow corn meal
4 teaspoons baking powder

*Easy to make.
Sweet and cheesy.*

- Mix all ingredients together
- Place in 9x11 pan.
- Preheat oven to 350°, reduce heat to 300° and bake for 1 hour.
Serves 10.

Cranberry Coffeecake

2 cups flour
1 teaspoon soda
1 teaspoon baking powder
½ teaspoon salt
¾ cup chopped nuts (optional)
½ cup butter

1 cup sugar
2 eggs
1 can (16 ounces) whole cranberry sauce
1 teaspoon almond extract
1 cup sour cream

Glaze:
¾ cup powdered sugar
2 tablespoons warm water

¼ teaspoon almond extract
¼ teaspoon vanilla

- Cream butter and sugar together.
- Add eggs one at a time. Add almond extract.
- Add dry ingredients alternating with the sour cream.
- Grease and flour bundt cake pan. Sprinkle bottom of pan with nuts.
- Pour in ⅓ of batter. Spread ½ can of cranberry sauce. Continue with ⅓ batter, ½ cranberry sauce, and end with the last ⅓ of batter on top.
- Bake 50-55 minutes at 350°.
- Cool thoroughly before removing from pan. Drizzle with glaze.
Glaze:
- Mix all ingredients together and drizzle over cool coffeecake.
Serves 12.

Mini Orange Muffins

½ cup butter
1 cup sugar
2 eggs
1 teaspoon baking soda
1 cup buttermilk

2 cups flour
grated zest of 2 oranges
juice of 2 oranges
½ cup golden raisins
1 cup brown sugar

- In a large bowl cream butter and sugar.
- Add eggs. Beat until well mixed.
- Dissolve baking soda in buttermilk. Add to mixture alternately with flour.
- Add orange zest and raisins.
- Fill well buttered tiny tart tins ¾ full. Bake at 400° for 15 minutes. Remove immediately and keep warm.
- In a small bowl mix orange juice and brown sugar. Pour 1 teaspoon over each warm muffin and top with zest.
Makes 24.

Poppyseed Bread

3 eggs
1½ cups milk
1⅛ cups oil
2¼ cups sugar
2 tablespoons poppyseeds
1½ teaspoons vanilla

1½ teaspoons almond extract
1½ teaspoons butter extract
3 cups sifted flour, measured
   after sifting
1½ teaspoons salt
1½ teaspoons baking powder

Glaze:

¼ cup orange juice
¾ cup sugar
1½ teaspoons vanilla

1½ teaspoons almond extract
1½ teaspoons butter extract

- Mix eggs, milk, oil, and sugar with a fork.
- Add poppyseeds, vanilla, almond extract, and butter extract.
- Add flour, salt, and baking powder. Beat thoroughly by hand.
- Grease and flour 2 loaf pans (8") or 1 bundt pan. Bake at 350° for 45 minutes or until toothpick comes out clean. Cool 10 minutes (45 for bundt).

Glaze:
- Mix glaze ingredients in a small sauce pan. Heat to dissolve sugar.
- Pour glaze over warm bread.
Serves 10-12.

Rhubarb Coffeecake

1½ cups brown sugar
½ cup margarine
2 eggs
1 cup buttermilk
2 cups flour

1 teaspoon soda
1 teaspoon vanilla
2 cups rhubarb, cut in ½"
   pieces

Topping:

½ cup sugar

1 teaspoon cinnamon

- Cream brown sugar and margarine in a large bowl.
- Beat in eggs.
- Add dry ingredients alternately with buttermilk, beginning and ending with dry.
- Add vanilla and fold in rhubarb.
- Pour into 9x13 pan and sprinkle with topping.
- Bake in a 350° oven for 35-40 minutes.
Serves 12.

Roquefort Wafers

1 cup self-rising flour
½ cup firm butter
2 ounces Roquefort cheese

2 ounces sharp Cheddar
* cheese, shredded*
½ cup sesame seeds
cucumber slices

- Sift flour and cut in butter until mixture resembles coarse crumbs.
- Crumble in cheeses, and mix ingredients with hands to form a dough. Cover and refrigerate.
- Place sesame seeds in dry skillet. Stir over medium heat until golden. Cool.
- Shape chilled dough into 36 equal balls. Toss each ball in sesame seeds, pressing balls flat to coat well.
- Arrange balls on greased baking sheets. Press lightly with a fork.
- Bake 10 minutes at 400° until golden around edges. Cool and store in airtight container.
- Garnish with cucumber slices.
Serves 18.

Banana Chocolate Chip Muffins

3 ripe bananas, mashed
2 eggs
1 cup sugar
¾ cup butter, melted
5 tablespoons buttermilk

2 teaspoons baking soda
¼ teaspoon salt
1 cup flour
¾ cup chocolate chips
1 cup roasted pecan pieces

- Mix the bananas, sugar and eggs together.
- Add butter after it has cooled.
- Mix flour, salt and baking soda. Add to banana mixture. Add buttermilk.
- Roast pecans on a cookie sheet in a 350° oven for 10 minutes.
- Stir in pecan pieces and chocolate chips.
- Spoon into muffin tins. Bake at 300° for 40 minutes.
Makes 12-16 muffins.

Spicy Buttermilk Coffeecake

2¼ cups flour
½ teaspoon salt
2 teaspoons cinnamon
¼ teaspoon ginger
1 cup brown sugar
¾ cup white sugar
¾ cup corn oil

1 cup walnuts or pecans,
* chopped*
1 teaspoon baking soda
1 teaspoon baking powder
1 egg, beaten
1 cup buttermilk

- Mix together in a large bowl the flour, salt, 1 teaspoon cinnamon, ginger, brown sugar, white sugar, and oil.
- Reserve ¾ cup of this mixture. Add to this ¾ cup the nuts and the additional 1 teaspoon cinnamon. Set aside.
- To the remaining mixture add baking soda, baking powder, egg, and buttermilk. Mix to combine (small lumps in the batter are OK).
- Pour batter into a well greased 9x13x2 pan. Sprinkle topping evenly on top.
- Bake at 350° for 40-45 minutes.
  Serves 8-10.

Another super recipe from Arcadia Farms in Scottsdale.

Brunches

Mushroom and Zucchini Frittata

1½ cups mushrooms, sliced
1½ cups zucchini, chopped
½ cup green pepper, chopped
¼ cup red pepper, chopped
¾ cup onion, chopped
1 large clove garlic, minced
1½ tablespoons vegetable oil
6 eggs, beaten
¼ cup milk

1 pound light cream cheese, diced
1½ cups Cheddar cheese, shredded
2 cups Italian or French bread, crusts removed
¾ teaspoon salt
¼ teaspoon pepper
¼ teaspoon paprika

- Sauté garlic and onion in oil. Add peppers, mushrooms and zucchini. Stir until zucchini is crisp-tender. Cool.
- Beat eggs with milk, salt, pepper, and paprika. Add bread, cream cheese and Cheddar cheese. Combine with vegetable mixture and mix well.
- Pour into oiled 10" springform pan. Bake at 350° for 1 hour, or until set in center.
- Cool 15 minutes before cutting into wedges.
  Serves 8.

Breakfast Burros

The key to this recipe is to use fresh, soft, warm tortillas. You can warm a few at a time in the microwave. Cover them with a damp paper towel and microwave on high for 15-30 seconds depending on the number of tortillas.
For a lower cholesterol version, use turkey sausage and eggbeaters.

1 package (12 ounces) pork sausage
½ cup green pepper, diced
4-6 green onions, sliced and using white part only

1 tomato, diced
4 eggs, beaten
1 cup thick and chunky salsa
8 medium flour tortillas
1 ripe avocado, diced

- Brown sausage over medium heat. Drain. Add green onions, peppers, and tomatoes. Sauté until soft. Set aside.
- In the same skillet, add eggs and scramble until firm. Add sausage mixture to eggs and mix together.
- Place ⅛ of mixture in center of warmed flour tortilla. Add salsa and avocado pieces on top of sausage mixture. Fold bottom edge of the tortilla over the mixture and roll into a cylinder shape.
  Serves 6-8.

Fiesta Corn Tamale Torte

Meat Filling:

2 tablespoons olive oil
1 medium onion, chopped
1-1½ pounds lean ground beef
4 large cloves garlic, minced

1 can (15 ounces) tomato sauce
¼ cup dry red wine
4½ teaspoons chili powder
salt and pepper to taste

Corn Bread:

3 eggs
1½ cups sour cream
1 cup milk
1 teaspoon sugar
1 can (7 ounces) chili salsa
1¼ cups yellow corn meal
1½ cups all purpose flour
1 teaspoon baking powder
1 teaspoon baking soda

1 teaspoon salt
several dashes of hot pepper
  sauce
1½ cans (12 ounces) corn with
  green and red peppers,
  drained
2½ cups Monterey Jack cheese,
  shredded
1 can (4 ounces) green chilies

This torte may be covered and refrigerated up to 2 days or frozen. Defrost at room temperature and reheat covered at 350° for 30 minutes or until heated through.

Meat Filling:
- Sauté onion in oil until soft.
- Add meat and garlic. Cook, stirring to break up meat, until it loses its red color. Drain.
- Stir in tomato sauce, wine, chili powder, salt, and pepper.
- Cook over moderately high heat, uncovered, stirring often until the liquid has evaporated, approximately 15-20 minutes. Set aside to cool.

Corn Bread:
- Whisk the eggs until frothy.
- Whisk in sour cream and milk.
- Add sugar, salsa, cornmeal, flour, baking powder, soda, salt, and hot pepper sauce. Whisk until combined.
- Stir in corn, cheese and green chilies.
- Generously butter the bottom and sides of springform pan. Wrap the outside of pan with foil, extending 2" above top to form a collar.
- Pour half the cornbread batter into the pan and spread evenly. Spoon meat over and spread gently to form an even layer. Top with remaining cornbread.
- Bake in center of 350° oven for 75-85 minutes or until golden brown and a sharp knife inserted into the center comes out clean.
- Remove from oven and let sit at room temperature for 20 minutes before serving.
- Serve with salsa and sour cream on the side.
Serves 6-8.

Tomato Herb Tart

If you are in a hurry, you can use prepared pie crust.

For a change, layer thin slices of ham between the cheese and tomatoes for a savory taste.

Crust:

1 cup flour
¼ teaspoon salt
¼ cup butter, chilled

2 tablespoons Crisco
3-4 tablespoons ice water

Filling:

¼-½ cup loosely packed parsley leaves, preferably Italian, minced
2-3 garlic cloves, peeled
½ cup olive oil
1 tablespoon fresh basil, chopped or 1 teaspoon dried
1 teaspoon dried oregano leaves

1 teaspoon dried thyme leaves
pinch of sugar
salt and pepper to taste
8 small Italian tomatoes, cored and ends cut flat
½ pound Mozzarella cheese, thinly sliced
¼-⅓ cup Dijon mustard

Crust:
- Stir flour and salt together in the bowl of a food processor fitted with a metal blade.
- Process butter and shortening into flour until mixture resembles coarse meal.
- Add ice water until dough begins to form a ball. Wrap in plastic wrap and thoroughly chill.

Filling:
- Mince parsley in food processor for 10 seconds. With the machine running, add garlic and process until minced.
- Add the oil, basil, oregano, thyme, salt, pepper, and sugar. Process for 5 seconds. Remove the metal blade and insert the medium slicing disc.
- Place the tomatoes cut side down in the feed tube and process using light pressure. Transfer the tomatoes and marinade to a bowl.
- Cover and refrigerate at least 6 hours, or overnight. Turn bowl once or twice.
- Roll out dough on a lightly floured surface into a 12" circle. Place into a 9" pie plate and flute edges.
- Spread the mustard evenly over the crust. Cover the bottom with the cheese and then place tomatoes (without marinade) in concentric circles.
- Bake at 400° for 30-45 minutes. Remove and let stand for at least 10 minutes.
  Serves 4-6.

Triple Cheese Bake

5 cups soft bread cubes
3 tablespoons melted butter
1½ cups Swiss cheese,
* shredded*
¼ cup Monterey Jack cheese,
* shredded*
1 pound bacon, cooked,
* drained and crumbled*

8 eggs
1⅔ cups milk
¼ cup white wine
2 whole green onions, minced
1 tablespoon brown mustard
½ cup sour cream
½ cup Parmesan cheese, grated

Outstanding brunch item and great on a buffet.

- Spread bread cubes on bottom of greased 9x13 pan. Drizzle butter over bread.
- Sprinkle with Swiss and Jack cheeses. Add bacon.
- Whisk together eggs, milk, wine, onions, and mustard. Pour over mixture in baking dish. Cover with foil and refrigerate at least 6 hours. Can keep up to 24 hours.
- Let sit at room temperature for 30 minutes before baking. Cover and bake in a 325° oven for 1 hour, or until set.
- Combine sour cream and Parmesan cheese. Spread over baked mixture. Leave uncovered and return to oven until crusty and lightly browned, about 10 minutes.
  Serves 8.

Spinach/Mushroom Brunch Bake

Remember, this dish must be made ahead of time.

12 fresh croissants, cut into thirds, horizontally
6-8 cups fresh mushrooms, sliced
¼ cup sun dried tomatoes, chopped
½ teaspoon thyme
2 tablespoons fresh basil, chopped
½ onion, chopped
1 pound spinach, blanched and drained

⅓ cup bacon, cooked and crumbled
½ pound ricotta cheese
⅔ cup Parmesan cheese, grated
4 ounces Mozzarella cheese, shredded
6 eggs
½ cup unsalted butter
2 cups milk
½ teaspoon pepper
1 teaspoon salt
¼ teaspoon nutmeg

- Place one-third of croissants into buttered baking dish, crust side down.
- Sauté mushrooms in 3-4 tablespoons butter until softened. Stir in tomatoes and herbs. Set aside.
- In the same skillet, melt remaining butter and sauté onion until soft. Stir in spinach, bacon, ricotta and ⅓ cup of Parmesan.
- Spread this mixture over croissants in a 9x13 baking dish. Cover with another third of croissants, crust side down.
- Spread mushroom mixture on top. Sprinkle with Mozzarella and place remaining croissants on top.
- Mix eggs with milk, pepper, nutmeg, and salt. Pour on top of casserole and press down on croissants so all pieces are moist. Cover and refrigerate for one or two days.
- Sprinkle with remaining Parmesan. Drizzle with some melted butter and bake at 375° for 45 minutes until brown.
  Serves 8-12.

Pancho Villa's Eggs

1 can (4 ounces) green chilies
6 eggs
⅔ cup milk
1 teaspoon sugar
1 teaspoon salt
1½ cups Cheddar cheese,
  shredded

1½ cups Monterey Jack cheese,
  shredded
1 package (3 ounces) cream
  cheese, cut in cubes
⅔ cup cottage cheese
½ cup flour
1 teaspoon baking powder
cayenne pepper

*Wonderful served
with a spicy
sausage on the
side.*

- Combine eggs, milk, sugar, and salt. Beat until frothy.
- Blend in cream cheese and cottage cheese.
- Combine flour and baking powder. Stir into egg mixture.
- Spread ½ chilies on bottom of greased 8-9" pan. Cover with ½ Cheddar cheese and ½ Jack cheese. Sprinkle remaining chilies over cheese. Cover with remaining cheese except for small amount for top.
- Pour egg mixture over cheese and sprinkle with extra cheeses. Add pepper to taste.
- Bake 40 minutes in 325° oven. Let stand 5 minutes before serving. **Serves 4-6.**

Sausage Enchiladas

2 packages (12 ounces) sage
  bulk sausage
1 large onion, finely chopped
1 can (8 ounces) chopped
  green chilies

4 eggs
1 pound Monterey Jack cheese,
  grated
2 cups white sauce
snack size flour tortillas

- Brown sausage with the onion. Pour off excess grease.
- Whip eggs and add to sausage mixture. Scramble.
- Soften tortillas in sealed bag in microwave for 1½ minutes.
- Put sausage mixture with a little cheese in each tortilla and roll. Place seam side down in a greased 13x9 pan.
- Can be prepared to this stage, and kept in refrigerator up to a week.
- To serve make a simple white sauce and pour over the tortillas. Sprinkle with more cheese and green chilies.
- Heat for 25 minutes in a 350° oven. **Serves 10-12.**

Rellenos Soufflé

*2 cans (27 ounces) whole green
　chilies, drained
¾ pound Monterey Jack
　cheese, cut into 18 strips
⅓ pound sharp Cheddar
　cheese, shredded*

*8 eggs, separated
1⅓ cups evaporated milk
1 teaspoon salt
1 teaspoon pepper
2 tablespoons flour*

- Preheat oven to 350°.
- Stuff all of the green chilies with the cheese strips. Place them side by side in an ungreased 9x13 baking pan.
- Beat egg whites until stiff.
- Beat egg yolks, milk, salt, pepper, and flour until mixed.
- Carefully fold in egg whites.
- Sprinkle shredded Cheddar cheese over stuffed chilies. Pour egg mixture on top. Bake 30 minutes or until lightly browned on top. **Serves 6-8.**

Spinach Quiche with Mushroom Sauce

*8" pie shell, baked for 10
 minutes*
*1¼ cups fresh spinach or 1 box
 (10 ounces) frozen, chopped
 and cooked 3-4 minutes*
2 tablespoons onion, chopped
2 tablespoons butter

½ teaspoon salt
⅛ teaspoon ground pepper
generous pinch nutmeg
3 eggs
1½ cups heavy cream
½ teaspoon ground pepper
¼ cup Swiss cheese, grated

Mushroom Sauce:
½ cup mushrooms, sliced
2 tablespoons butter
2 tablespoons flour
¾ cup chicken stock

½ cup heavy cream
salt
sherry

- Cook spinach. Drain.
- Sauté onion in butter for 2 minutes. Add spinach and heat for several minutes.
- Add salt, pepper, and nutmeg.
- Combine eggs, cream, and pepper. Blend well. Add spinach and cheese mixture. Salt and pepper to taste.
- Pour into pie shell. Dot with 1 tablespoon butter. Bake in upper oven for 40-45 minutes at 375° or until set.

Mushroom Sauce:
- Sauté mushrooms in butter. Add flour, stock, and cream. Season with salt and sherry.
  Serves 6-8.

Poultry

Chicken Acapulco

8 chicken breast halves, boned
  and skinned
1 can (7 ounces) diced green
  chilies divided into 8
  portions
¼ pound Monterey Jack
  cheese, cut into 8 strips

½ cup fine dry bread crumbs
¼ cup grated Parmesan cheese
1 tablespoon chili powder
½ teaspoon salt
¼ teaspoon cumin
¼ teaspoon pepper
6 tablespoons butter, melted

Tomato Sauce:

1 can (15 ounces) tomato
  sauce
½ teaspoon cumin
⅓ cup sliced green onions

salt
pepper
hot pepper sauce

- Pound chicken pieces to ¼ inch thickness.
- Place chilies and Jack cheese strip in center of each chicken piece. Roll up and tuck ends under.
- Combine bread crumbs, Parmesan cheese, chili powder, salt, cumin, and pepper.
- Dip each stuffed chicken breast in shallow bowl of 6 tablespoons melted butter. Roll in crumb mixture.
- Place chicken seam side down in oblong baking dish. Drizzle with a little melted butter.
- Cover and chill for 4 hours or overnight.
- Bake uncovered at 400° for 20 minutes or until done.
- Serve with Tomato Sauce or salsa.

Tomato Sauce:

- Combine tomato sauce, cumin, and green onions. Add hot pepper sauce, salt and pepper to taste.
- Heat through.
  Serves 8.

Chicken Balsamic

2 tablespoons butter
1 tablespoon oil
4 large chicken breast halves,
   boned and skinned
½ pound mushrooms, sliced

⅓ cup balsamic vinegar
6 tablespoons butter, room
   temperature, cut in 6 pieces
2 teaspoons fresh thyme
cooked fettuccini

- Sauté chicken breasts in the butter and oil until brown on both sides. Cover pan and continue cooking for 5 minutes over low heat. Remove to warm platter.
- Sauté mushrooms in pan for 5 minutes. Add to chicken platter and keep warm.
- Add vinegar to pan and reduce sauce to half. Whisk in butter, one piece at a time. Add thyme, salt and pepper to taste.
- Spoon sauce over chicken and mushrooms and serve over fettuccini.
  Serves 4.

Cumberland Chicken

½ cup Parmesan cheese
2 cups seasoned bread crumbs
3 tablespoons sesame seeds

4 chicken breasts, split
½ cup melted butter

Sauce:
1 cup red current jelly
1 can (6 ounces) frozen orange
   juice, thawed
4 tablespoons wine or sherry

1 teaspoon dry mustard
⅛ teaspoon ground ginger
¼ teaspoon hot pepper sauce

- Mix cheese, crumbs and seeds.
- Dip chicken pieces in butter, then crumbs. Place in shallow pan.
- Drizzle remaining butter over chicken pieces.
- Bake at 350° for 30-45 minutes.
Sauce:
- Combine all ingredients and simmer until smooth. Serve with chicken.
  Serves 8.

Dijon Chicken Wraps

4 ounces Blue cheese
12 ounces soft cream cheese
¾ pound Gruyère cheese, grated
10 half chicken breasts, skinned, boned, and pounded thin

1 jar (10 ounces) Dijon mustard
6 eggs-beaten
1 cup white flour
1 cup whole wheat flour
16 ounces herb seasoned stuffing
2 quarts Wesson oil

- Combine Blue cheese with cream cheese. Mix well.
- Form cheese mixture into 10 balls. Roll each ball in Gruyère cheese.
- Place balls in freezer until firm, ½ hour.
- Spread one side of chicken breast with Dijon mustard. Place a cheese ball in center. Wrap the chicken around the ball. Secure with a tooth pick.
- Roll chicken in flour, dip in beaten egg, and roll in stuffing.
- Deep fry in hot oil (400°) for 10 seconds. Remove and drain.
- Transfer to baking dish. Bake at 350° for 30 minutes. Remove toothpicks before serving.
Serves 10.

Grilled Margarita Chicken

4 boneless, skinless chicken breasts
Marinade:
⅔ cup olive oil
½ cup fresh squeezed lime juice

¼ cup tequila
⅛ cup triple sec
¼ cup fresh cilantro, chopped

- Mix together marinade in non-reactive bowl.
- Marinate chicken for 1-2 hours at room temperature or 4 hours in refrigerator.
- Grill chicken over hot coals 10-15 minutes, turning 3-4 times.
- Baste liberally with reserved marinade.
Serves 4.

Parmesan Chicken

*6 chicken breast halves, boned
  and skinned*
*½ cup freshly grated Parmesan
  cheese*
¼ cup dry bread crumbs
salt and pepper
*1 tablespoon chopped fresh
  tarragon*

*1 tablespoon chopped fresh
  thyme*
1 tablespoon butter
2 tablespoons olive oil
½ cup white wine
¼ cup chicken broth

- Season chicken breasts with salt and pepper. Dredge breasts in mixture of ¼ cup cheese, bread crumbs, tarragon, and thyme.
- Heat butter and olive oil. Sauté chicken over medium heat until browned on both sides. Transfer to baking dish.
- In same skillet, add wine and chicken broth. Bring to a boil, cook for 10 minutes until reduced. Pour over chicken. Sprinkle with remaining cheese.
- Bake uncovered in a preheated oven at 325° for 20-25 minutes. **Serves 6.**

Imperial Chicken

2 cups dry bread crumbs
¼ cup fresh parsley, minced
1 clove garlic, minced
1½ teaspoons salt
⅛ teaspoon pepper
1-2 cups melted butter

1¼ tablespoons Dijon mustard
*1 teaspoon Worchestershire
  sauce*
*6-8 chicken breast halves,
  boned and skinned*
parsley sprigs

- Combine crumbs, parsley, garlic, salt, and pepper.
- Combine melted butter, mustard, and Worchestershire.
- Dip chicken first in butter mixture, then in crumbs.
- Place chicken in baking pan. Sprinkle with leftover butter mixture.
- Bake, uncovered at 350°, for 45 minutes or until tender. **Serves 6-8.**

Santa Fe Kiev

4 boneless chicken breast
  halves
4 tablespoons butter
2 ounces cream cheese
2 ounces Goat cheese

1 tablespoon minced onion
1 clove garlic, minced
2 Anaheim chilies, cut into
  strips and chopped

Sauce:
1 cup sour cream

1 can (4 ounces) chopped
  green chilies

- Sauté onion, garlic and Anaheim green chilies in butter until onions are transparent.
- Mix the cream cheese and Goat cheese together.
- Pound the breasts until flat. Spoon equal amounts of sautéed ingredients evenly over them.
- Place 1 tablespoon cheese mixture on each breast. Roll up tightly and secure with toothpicks.
- Place in pie pan, cover, and refrigerate for 8-24 hours. Bake at 350° for 30 minutes, or until done.

Sauce:
- Reserve pan drippings. Combine with sour cream and green chilies for a tasty sauce.
Serves 4.

Luscious Chicken Medallions

The orange and green of the vegetables make these medallions really beautiful to present.

8 chicken breast halves, boned
  and skinned
2-3 carrots, cut into 8 sticks
  and blanched

2-3 stalks celery, cut into 8
  sticks and blanched
8 sticks Dolfino or Swiss cheese
Parmesan cheese

- Flatten each chicken breast. Stuff each with 1 stick of cheese, carrot and celery. Sprinkle with Parmesan.
- Tightly roll up each breast (jelly roll style). Roll each breast up in saran wrap, securely tying a knot at each end as you would a "sausage".
- Place into boiling water. Boil uncovered for 10-12 minutes.
- Unwrap chicken rolls, slice and serve with your favorite sauce.
Serves 8.

Chicken Breasts Marsala

6 chicken breast halves,
  skinned, boned and lightly
  flattened
salt and pepper to taste
¾ cup herb seasoned stuffing
  mix

½ an apple, peeled and
  coarsely grated
⅓ cup pecans, chopped
1½ tablespoons melted butter
apple juice
flour

Sauce:
⅓ cup onion, finely chopped
4 tablespoons butter
½ pound mushrooms, sliced
¼ cup Marsala

1 tablespoon flour
1 cup half and half
salt and pepper to taste

- Combine herb stuffing mix, apple, pecans, and butter. Add enough apple juice to hold mixture together. Season with salt and pepper.
- Divide into 6 equal parts. Place one part in center of each chicken breast.
- Roll up jelly roll style, tucking in edges, using your fingers to seal.
- Roll lightly in flour and in melted butter.
- Place in shallow oblong baking pan. Sprinkle with paprika.
- Bake 400° for 20 minutes, or until done.

Sauce:
- Sauté onion in butter until soft. Add mushrooms and sauté until tender.
- Add flour and stir. Add half and half and Marsala. Cook until sauce thickens.
- Spoon sauce on top to serve.
  Serves 6.

Chicken in Champagne Cream Sauce

4 chicken breast halves
1 teaspoon thyme
1 teaspoon seasoned salt
dash of garlic powder

6 tablespoons butter
⅔ cup champagne
2 teaspoons flour
1 cup whipping cream

- Sprinkle chicken breasts with seasonings.
- Brown chicken in butter, add champagne, and cover.
- Simmer 30-40 minutes until chicken is tender. Remove from pan.
- Using a wire whisk, thicken sauce with flour. Stir in cream and heat. Serve over chicken.
  Serves 4.

Chicken Marbella

Serve with wild rice. Also delicious served cold.

4 chickens, 2½ pounds each, quartered
1 head garlic, pureed
¼ cup dried oregano
coarse black pepper to taste
½ cup red wine vinegar
½ cup virgin olive oil

1 cup pitted prunes
½ cup pitted Spanish olives
½ cup capers with a bit of juice
6 bay leaves
1 cup brown sugar
1 cup white wine
¼ cup fresh cilantro, chopped

- Combine chicken, garlic, oregano, pepper, vinegar, olive oil, prunes, olives, capers, and bay leaves. Cover and marinate in refrigerator overnight.
- Arrange chicken in single layer in 1 or 2 shallow baking pans. Pour marinade over top. Sprinkle with brown sugar. Pour white wine around chicken.
- Bake for 50 minutes to 1 hour in 350° oven, basting frequently.
- Transfer chicken, prunes, olives, and capers to serving platter. Moisten with pan juices. Sprinkle generously with cilantro.
- Reduce remaining juices and serve as a sauce.
  Serves 12-16.

Portuguese Chicken

This chicken dish has a nice rich color and is very flavorful. The marinade paste will keep for weeks in the refrigerator.

Serve with stuffed, sliced ripe olives on top of each breast.

6-8 chicken breast halves, boned and skinned
2 large garlic cloves, minced
1 large bay leaf, crumbled
2 teaspoons paprika

2 teaspoons salt
¼ teaspoon crushed dried red chili peppers
¼ teaspoon black pepper
2 tablespoons olive oil

- Mix all ingredients together EXCEPT the chicken. It will be in paste form.
- At least 2-3 hours before cooking time, brush both sides of chicken with the paste.
- Cover with plastic wrap and refrigerate for 30 minutes.
- Remove from refrigerator and let sit for 30 minutes before cooking.
- Grill chicken until done.
  Serves 6-8.

Chicken in Mustard Sauce

1 tablespoon oil
4 chicken breast halves, boned,
  skinned and cut into 1½"
  pieces
⅓ cup dry white wine
½ cup heavy cream

1 tablespoon Dijon mustard
¼ teaspoon tarragon
dash of cayenne pepper
1 tablespoon lemon juice
salt and pepper to taste

- Sauté chicken in oil over medium high heat until golden brown on each side, about 4 minutes. Remove.
- Add wine to pan. Bring to a boil, scraping the bottom.
- Whisk in remaining ingredients. Reduce mixture until thick enough to coat a spoon.
- Add chicken pieces. Lower heat to simmer. Cover and simmer for 5 minutes.
  Serves 4.

Chicken Piccata

4 chicken breast halves, boned
½ cup flour
1 tablespoon olive oil
2 tablespoons unsalted butter
¼ cup Madeira wine
½ cup lemon juice

4 tablespoons capers
½ teaspoon freshly ground
  pepper
½ teaspoon paprika
½ teaspoon cayenne pepper

- Pound chicken breast halves between two sheets of wax paper until ¼ inch thickness.
- Mix flour, pepper, paprika, and cayenne pepper in large plastic bag. Shake chicken in the bag. Shake off excess.
- Sauté chicken over high heat in hot oil and butter. Brown for about 3 minutes per side. Remove.
- Add wine, lemon juice, and capers to skillet. Bring to a boil. Pour sauce over chicken with 1 tablespoon of capers on each. Garnish with pepper.
  Serves 4.

Marinated Chicken

6 chicken breast halves, boned
   and skinned
2 cups sour cream
1/4 cup lemon juice
2 tablespoons Worchestershire
   sauce
2 teaspoons celery salt
2 teaspoons paprika

4 cloves garlic, crushed
1 teaspoon salt
1/2 teaspoon pepper
2 cups seasoned bread crumbs
1/2 cup fresh Parmesan cheese,
   grated
1 stick butter, melted

- Combine all ingredients EXCEPT chicken, crumbs, Parmesan cheese, and butter.
- Marinate chicken overnight in sauce.
- Mix together crumbs and cheese. Roll chicken in mixture. Drizzle with melted butter.
- Bake 45 minutes at 350°.
  Serves 6.

Baked Chicken with Peaches

8-12 chicken thighs
1 teaspoon salt
1/2 teaspoon pepper
1 cup fresh orange juice
4 tablespoons Dijon mustard
1/4 cup orange honey
1/4 cup margarine, melted

1 clove garlic, crushed
1 tablespoon soy sauce
3 tablespoons dry sherry
1/2 teaspoon ginger
4 fresh peaches, peeled, halved,
   and pitted

- Season chicken with salt and pepper. Bake, uncovered in a 350° oven, for 30 minutes.
- Combine remaining ingredients EXCEPT peaches. Baste chicken with orange honey sauce. Bake another 30 minutes basting frequently.
- Arrange peach halves around chicken, baste with sauce and continue baking another 15 minutes or until chicken is tender.
- Serve extra sauce on side.
  Serves 4-6.

Chicken Phyllo Casserole

½ cup sweet butter
4 boned, skinned whole
  chicken breasts, cut in 1"
  cubes
⅓ cup Dijon mustard
2 tablespoons minced fresh
  tarragon or ⅔ teaspoon
  dried
1½ cups heavy cream
1 red bell pepper, julienned

1 green bell pepper, julienned
5 fresh sliced mushrooms
½ medium onion, diced
1 tablespoon dry sherry
2 tablespoons white
  Worcestershire sauce
white pepper and salt
¾ cup sweet butter melted
phyllo pastry sheets

*Colorful, tasty
dish that is won-
derful to serve to
company.*

- Melt ¼ cup butter in large pan. Sprinkle chicken with salt and pepper. Sauté 5 minutes until white throughout.
- Transfer to plate and keep warm.
- Whisk mustard in chicken drippings. Add tarragon. Reduce slightly. Fold in cream. Reduce heat to low.
- Simmer sauce until thickened and reduced by ¼. Add sherry and Worcestershire sauce.
- Pour over chicken and toss to coat. Set aside.
- Melt remaining ¼ cup butter in fry pan. Sauté onions and mushrooms until soft. Drain any liquid. Add peppers. Sauté briefly to keep them crisp. Set aside.
- Brush a medium baking dish with melted butter. Place one phyllo sheet in dish letting edges overlap sides of dish. Pat to fit sides.
- Repeat 4 more times, brushing with butter between each.
- Fill casserole with chicken mix and then layer pepper mixture on top. Make sure all peppers lay flat.
- Layer 5 more phyllo sheets on top, brushing with butter between each. Trim excess phyllo to 1 inch from dish edge. Fold edges of sheets into dish brushing thoroughly with butter to keep in place.
- Bake at 350° for 25-30 minutes or until golden brown.
  Serves 8.

Chicken and Ham Roll-ups

4 cups cooked chicken
20 thin slices of ham, honey
  cured
¼ cup butter
1 pound mushrooms, sliced
4 tablespoons flour

1 cup chicken broth
1½ cups sour cream
½ pound Gjetost cheese,
  shredded
chopped parsley

- Divide chicken into 20 equal portions. Wrap each portion in 1 slice of ham. Place rolls seam side down in a 9x13 pan.
- Melt 2 tablespoons butter in skillet. Add mushrooms and cook until limp. Stir in remaining butter until melted. Add flour. Cook, stirring until sauce boils and thickens.
- Remove from heat. Stir in cheese until it begins to melt. Spoon over filled rolls. Cover and chill.
- Bake, covered, in a 400° oven for 35 minutes or until bubbling.
- Sprinkle with parsley. Use extra sauce from pan as an accompaniment.
  Serves 10-12.

Artichoke Chicken Casserole

Substitute Parmesan cheese for bread crumbs, or use equal parts of each.

1 jar marinated artichokes (24
  ounces)
4 cups cooked chicken breast
2 cans (10¾ ounces) cream of
  chicken soup
½ cup milk
1 cup mayonnaise
1 teaspoon lemon juice

½ teaspoon curry powder
1¼ cups sharp Cheddar cheese,
  shredded
½ pound mushrooms
2 cups cooked rice
¾ cup seasoned bread crumbs
2 tablespoons melted butter
Parmesan cheese, optional

- Drain and quarter artichokes. Place in bottom of a 9x13 pan.
- Layer rice and chicken over artichokes.
- Mix the soup, milk, mayonnaise, mushrooms, lemon juice, curry, and ¾ cup of cheese together.
- Pour over the chicken and artichokes. Sprinkle the remaining cheese on top.
- Toast bread crumbs in melted butter, toss with Parmesan cheese (if using), and spread on top of the casserole.
- Bake 350° for 30 minutes.
- Can be made the night before and refrigerated. Add the bread crumbs when you are ready to bake the casserole.
  Serves 8-10.

Chicken Chimichangas

6 cooked chicken breast halves, boned, skinned and cubed
2 cups Cheddar cheese, grated
2 cups Monterey Jack cheese, grated
1 cup diced green onion

1 can (4 ounces) diced green chilies
1 cup sour cream
12 (12") flour tortillas
oil to brown

- Mix chicken, cheeses, onion, chilies, and sour cream. It is easiest to do this with your hands.
- Put ⅔ cup of the mixture in the center of each tortilla and roll up.
- Cook the rolled tortillas, seam side down first, in ½ - 1 inch of hot oil until tortillas are well browned on all sides.
- Serve hot with salsa, sour cream and/or guacamole on the side.
- These can be cooked ahead of time and frozen. Reheat on a brown paper lined cookie sheet in a 375° oven for 20-25 minutes.
  Serves 8, or can be cut into small pieces and served as hors d'oeuvres.

Red Chicken Enchilada Casserole

¾ cup onion, chopped
1 can (14 ounces) mild enchilada sauce
2 cans (10.4 ounces) chopped tomatoes
2 cans (4 ounces) chopped green chilies
½ cup almonds, sliced
3 cups Monterey Jack cheese, shredded

6-8 boneless chicken breast halves, cooked and cubed
10 corn tortillas (6"), torn into pieces
1 teaspoon ground cumin
1½ teaspoons garlic powder
½ teaspoon salt
2 teaspoons ground oregano

- Mix all the ingredients together EXCEPT the tortillas and cheese.
- Spray bottom of 13x9 baking dish with Pam.
- Alternate layers of tortillas, meat mixture and cheese.
- Bake at 350° for 30 minutes. Let cool for 10 minutes before serving. Top with chopped green onions.
  Serves 6-8.

Turkey with Raspberry Sauce

This raspberry sauce is also great on chicken or pork roast.

2-3 turkey tenderloins (about
   1½ pounds)
1 tablespoon lemon juice
1 tablespoon water
2 teaspoons soy sauce
1 package (10 ounces) frozen
   raspberries

1 tablespoon raspberry vinegar
½ cup orange juice
1 tablespoon arrowroot
2 tablespoons grated orange
   peel
½ pint fresh raspberries
4-6 orange slices

- Rinse turkey tenderloins, pat dry, and pierce on both sides with a fork.
- Combine lemon juice, water, and soy sauce. Marinate the turkey in sauce for at least 2 hours.
- Brown turkey in a non-stick pan coated with a vegetable spray. Brush with the marinade. Turn down the heat and simmer for 10 minutes on each side.
- Combine orange juice and arrowroot until smooth in a small sauce pan. Add the thawed raspberries, vinegar and orange peel to arrowroot mixture.
- Cook and stir until thick and bubbly; cook and stir 2 minutes more.
- Place turkey on serving platter. Cover with the raspberry sauce. Garnish with fresh raspberries and orange slices. Slice thinly to serve.
Serves 6-8.

Tortilla Sandwiches

A healthy, nutritious, colorful meal.

1 large flour tortilla
4 slices turkey breast
1 avocado, mashed
lemon juice
salt

2 green onions, chopped
2 tablespoons cilantro, chopped
1 small tomato, chopped
shredded lettuce or sprouts
shredded Cheddar cheese

- Mash avocado with lemon juice and salt.
- Lay tortilla flat and layer ingredients on top.
- Carefully roll into a tube. Trim off ends.
- Cut in half to make two sandwiches.
Serves 2.

Phoenix Treasures

Blessed with a dry, warm climate and encircled with mountains, Phoenix and its 21 surrounding communities combine to create the Valley of the Sun.

The U.S.'s eighth largest city, cosmopolitan yet casual, Phoenix is situated in the heart of the Sonoran Desert.

Known worldwide as a vacation destination, the area is a study in contrasts. Lush, relaxing resorts are close to upbeat galleries and museums. Performing arts companies thrive amid the steel high-rises of downtown, while a few miles away, Old West towns and horse shows beckon from spectacular desert terrain.

Glimpse a few of our treasures on the following pages—they speak of a lifestyle in harmony with nature and with a diverse cultural heritage.

City

Downtown Phoenix glints copper in the setting sun as it rises above the desert floor.

Bustling with corporate employees by day, concerned with economics and business ventures, the city does an about-face at sundown and draws the crowd like an entertainment magnet.

Choices seem unlimited, even overwhelming. A major symphony orchestra, regional theatre, opera, and ballet companies offer superb performances year-round. Guest artists and top performers share the stage with weekend city-wide festivals.

Turkey with Raspberry Sauce

Resorts

Prized by visitors and residents alike, the Phoenix metropolitan area boasts an assembly of world-class resorts second to none.

Championship golf courses and superb tennis facilities await! Guests may also choose the relaxed pampering of the spa or an energetic hike along desert trails—saddle up for a horseback ride through nearby mountains—lunch poolside with a scenic view of lushly landscaped and manicured grounds—follow with dinner at a five-star table or sample diverse ethnic cuisine.

Offered such great accommodations and superb service, guests are inclined to say "yes" again and again to the Valley of the Sun.

Spinach/Mushroom Brunch Bake

Architecture

Using the clay and raw materials of the desert, Sonoran natives protected themselves with simple thick-walled adobe shelters.

Today, a beautiful eclectic mix of structures populates the city. Southwestern, contemporary, and ranch-style homes create a neighborhood mix. And the Frank Lloyd Wright influence is present in many public buildings, such as the Biltmore Hotel, and the Gammage Center for the Performing Arts.

Always, this blend of shelter emphasizes our relaxed lifestyle and inclination to keep nature's beauty close at hand. "Bring the outdoors in" is the cornerstone of Phoenix architecture.

Phyllo Blossoms

Desert

Sage green saguaros and flat disks of prickly pear contrast with blue spikes of lupine and the yellow daisy-like blooms of the brittlebush to echo spring in the desert.

Far from being a barren wasteland, the Sonoran Desert is alive with color in every season, and always in spring.

During the months of March and April, wildflowers are rampant in mountain preserves and along roadways. Wildlife abounds too, especially in early morning hours. Visitors can glimpse roadrunners, quail, and lizards darting through cool bushes or an elf owl returning home to its cactus nest.

Picante Corn Casserole

Water

Fountains splash and pools beckon. On the outskirts of the city, float-trip enthusiasts glide past the riparian habitats of the Salt and Verde Rivers.

Upon casual glance, it seems that Phoenix has an abundance of water, but with an average rainfall of only seven inches per year, one cannot forget that Phoenix and the desert are one.

Residents are encouraged and educated to conserve. Xeriscaping (low-water-use plants) provides plenty of soothing green with minimal moisture. Through careful conservation, this lifegiving resource will remain an integral part of the Valley lifestyle.

Tart au Citron

Native Americans

Silent sentinels speak to us of past and present. Adding levity to a solemn rain dance, the Hopi Indian clown kachina (masked) dancer stands, boldly striped in black and white.

All of Arizona and especially the Gila and Salt River Valleys near Phoenix have been home to Native American tribes since ancient times. Constructing complex irrigation systems, the Hohokam were diverting river water to their crops long before Columbus sailed for the New World.

Today, festivals, ceremonials, and dances carefully preserve Native American culture. World-renowned museums, such as the Heard, beautifully exhibit the intricately designed pottery, basketry, and textiles that help tell the story of the Indian heritage.

Hearts of Palm Salad with
Tangy Lemon Dressing

Old West

From staged Old West shootouts and Pony Express riders retracing the mail route to colorful rodeos and costumed riders on horses in festival parades, cowboy lore lives on in Scottsdale and Phoenix.

Famed for his rugged individualism in Western films, the cowboy and his horse seem at one with nature, riding off into a spectacular Arizona sunset.

His touch is evident today, not only on the real working range, but also in the Southwestern influence mirrored in food, art, fashion, and interior design.

Caviar Pie

Courtesy of The Arizona Biltmore

Hank Saunders Adstock Photos

Courtesy of The Hyatt Regency Resort Scottsdale

Jerry Jacka, Elizabeth Abeyta

David Stoecklein Adstock Photos

Lonna Tucker Adstock Photos

Jerry Jacka

Entrees

Tenderloin of Beef with Tarragon Sauce

*1½ pounds beef tenderloin,
  room temperature*

*black pepper
3 tablespoons vegetable oil*

Tarragon Sauce:

½ cup olive oil
1½ teaspoons Dijon mustard
*1 teaspoon Worcestershire
  sauce*
2 tablespoons tarragon vinegar

2 tablespoons heavy cream
1 teaspoon egg yolk
*1 tablespoon fresh tarragon,
  chopped*
1 tablespoon scallions, minced

- Rub tenderloin with vegetable oil and coat with pepper. Brown on all sides in left-over oil.
- Roast in preheated 500° oven for 20 minutes. Meat thermometer should register 130°.
- Blend mustard, Worcestershire , vinegar, cream, and yolk in food processor.
- Add olive oil in stream while processing until emulsified. Remove to a mixing bowl and stir in tarragon and scallions.
- Slice tenderloins into ½" pieces and spoon sauce on top.
  Serves 6.

Beef Grand Marnier

2-4 pound beef tenderloin
1 cup Grand Marnier
1 cup barbeque sauce
1 package (8 ounces) sliced
  Jack cheese

2 teaspoons minced garlic
2 teaspoons minced onion
salt and pepper

- Place tenderloin in a loaf pan. Split middle slightly. Pour Grand Marnier over top, and then the BBQ sauce.
- Season with the minced garlic, onion, salt and pepper. Cover and let stand for 4-6 hours.
- Place pan on grill over hot coals. Cover and cook approximately 45 minutes. (Can be baked in oven for 1 hour at 350°.)
- Cover top with Jack cheese and cook until cheese melts. Remove, slice, and serve.
  Serves 6-8.

Sonoran Shredded Beef

2½ pound pork tenderloin
2½ pound roast beef
4 cloves crushed garlic
2 cans (8 ounces) green chilies
cayenne pepper to taste

diced, fresh jalapeños to taste
1½ cans cream of mushroom
  soup (10¾ ounces each)
black pepper to taste
1 cup sour cream

This can easily be made in a crock pot on low.

- Place pork and beef in a large pan with garlic, chilies, cayenne pepper, and jalapeños. Cover and cook in a 250° oven for at least 6 hours, or until meat falls apart.
- Mix in soup, black pepper, and sour cream.
- Cook another 1½ hours.
- Serve with warm tortillas or fold into burros. Top with guacamole.
  Serves 16.

Filet in Puff Pastry

Start this sauce in the morning. It is delicious and well worth the effort.

6 beef tenderloins, 6 ounces each
6 tablespoons unsalted butter
2 shallots, minced
1 pound mushrooms, finely chopped
4 tablespoons heavy cream

2 tablespoons parsley, chopped
1 pinch thyme
salt and pepper to taste
2 pounds frozen puff pastry, thawed as directed on package
1 egg, lightly beaten

Brown Sauce:

½ cup butter
2 onions, cut in large pieces
1 carrot, cut in large pieces
1 cup flour
8 cups beef stock
3 sprigs of parsley

1 stalk of celery
1 garlic clove, crushed
1 small bay leaf
pinch of thyme
¼ cup tomato puree

- Sauté tenderloins in 3 tablespoons butter for 30 seconds per side. Cool completely.
- Add remaining butter and cook shallots, mushrooms, and parsley until liquid evaporates.
- Add cream, salt, pepper and thyme. Cook until it resembles a thick puree. Cool.
- Preheat oven to 450°.
- Divide pastry into squares large enough to cover the tenderloins. Place a tenderloin in the center of the pastry, top with the mushroom mixture, and fold over.
- Seal the edges with egg wash. Bake 15-20 minutes, or until pastry is golden brown. Serve with brown sauce.

Brown Sauce:

- Sauté onion and carrot pieces in butter until onions are golden brown.
- Add flour and cook over low heat until the mixture is a rich brown.
- Remove from heat and add 3 cups heated beef stock. Stir well until combined.
- Add parsley, celery, garlic, bay leaf, and thyme. Cook over low heat, stirring until it thickens.
- Add 3 more cups heated beef stock and simmer sauce, stirring occasionally. Skim the froth as it comes to the surface. Cook 1-1½ hours.
- Add tomato puree. Cook for 5 minutes. Strain through a sieve into a bowl. Return the sauce to the pan and add 2 more cups hot beef stock. Simmer until reduced to about 4 cups.

Serves 6.

Italian Stuffed Eggplant

1 large eggplant
2 tablespoons olive oil
1 large onion, finely chopped
1½ pounds ground beef
4 eggs
1 cup Parmesan cheese
⅓ cup wine

1 can (28 ounces) crushed
  tomatoes
1 large clove garlic, mashed
1½ cups bread crumbs
½ teaspoon basil
½ teaspoon oregano
salt and pepper to taste

Slice thin and use as an appetizer too.

- Cut eggplant in half lengthwise.
- Scoop out pulp of eggplant. Simmer pulp with onion in olive oil until soft. Cool.
- Mix remaining ingredients EXCEPT tomatoes together.
- Add sautéed pulp and onions to mixture, and mix well.
- Fill eggplant shells with meat mixture.
- Put ½ of crushed tomatoes in bottom of baking pan. Place eggplant halves on top, and pour remaining tomatoes over top.
- Bake at 350° for 1½ hours.
  Serves 8.

Veal Strips with Artichokes

Try using chicken or turkey strips too.

¾ pound boneless veal, cut into
  ¼" slices
2 tablespoons flour
¼ teaspoon salt
⅛ teaspoon pepper
⅛ teaspoon paprika
1 jar (6 ounces) marinated
  artichoke hearts

1 medium onion, sliced
butter
¼ cup chicken broth
1 tablespoon lemon juice
½ cup sour cream
2 tablespoons Parmesan,
  grated
spinach noodles, cooked

- Trim and pound each piece of veal between 2 pieces of wax paper until ⅛" thick. Cut each piece into ¾" wide strips.
- Combine flour, salt, pepper, and paprika. Dredge veal strips in mixture.
- Drain artichoke liquid into 10" fry pan, reserving artichokes for garnish. Sauté veal strips in liquid until well browned, 3-5 minutes. Set aside.
- Add butter, if necessary, and sauté onions for 5 minutes.
- Add broth and stir to loosen bits. Stir in lemon juice, sour cream, cheese and veal strips. Heat and serve over spinach noodles.
  Serves 4.

Grilled Leg of Lamb

6-7 pound of leg of lamb
  (boned, butterflied, and
  trimmed of most fat)

Marinade:
1 cup ketchup
1 cup water
¼ cup Worcestershire sauce
¼ cup apple cider vinegar
¼ cup brown sugar

2-3 drops Tabasco
1 teaspoon celery salt
1 teaspoon chili powder
1 teaspoon salt

- Mix marinade ingredients and heat on low. Do not boil.
- Pour over lamb, cover and refrigerate for at least 24 hours.
- Grill on medium to low coals for 50-60 minutes, basting 4-6 times.
  Serves 6.

Moghul Lamb

5 pound leg of lamb, boned,
  rolled and tied
1 teaspoon seasoned salt
1 teaspoon pepper
2 teaspoons garlic, minced

1 cup chutney
1 yellow onion, sliced
¼ cup water
¼ cup honey

- Sprinkle lamb with salt, pepper, and spread on garlic.
- Spread lamb with 2 tablespoons chutney and top with onion.
- Place meat thermometer in roast. Place on a rack in a shallow pan.
- Bake at 325° for 2 hours. Drain off drippings.
- Mix remaining chutney with honey and water. Pour over lamb.
- Bake at 325° for 30 minutes longer or until thermometer registers 175°.
- Baste occasionally throughout cooking.
Serves 8.

Indian Lamb Kabobs

2 pounds boneless lamb,
  trimmed and cut into 2"
  cubes
1 teaspoon ground cumin
½ teaspoon tumeric
2 teaspoons salt
2 tablespoons ginger, finely
  chopped

½ cup onion, finely chopped
1 teaspoon garlic cloves, finely
  chopped
2 tablespoons fresh cilantro,
  finely chopped
½ cup plain yogurt

Various condiments which enhance this dish are: chutney, hard boiled eggs, raisins, slivered almonds, shredded fresh coconut, sliced green onions, chopped green pepper, and of course, rice.

- Combine the lamb, cumin, tumeric, salt and ginger in a glass or stainless steel bowl. Toss to coat the meat evenly.
- Add the onions, garlic, cilantro, and yogurt. Toss again to thoroughly mix.
- Cover loosely and marinate at room temperature for 4 hours or refrigerate for 6 hours.
- Broil or barbeque skewered meat (thread closely to preserve moistness) for 10 minutes in all. Test for doneness.
Serves 4.

Pork Loin Roast with Orange BBQ Sauce

The roast can also be baked in oven at 350° until done. Baste the same as on grill.

Pork roast-boneless or rib
1 can (6 ounces) frozen orange
  juice concentrate
¼ cup wine vinegar

2 tablespoons brown sugar,
  packed
2 tablespoons honey
2 teaspoons prepared mustard
2 teaspoons soy sauce

- Sprinkle roast with garlic salt and grill over coals for ½ hour.
- Combine remaining ingredients and stir over low heat until blended.
- Baste roast with orange sauce, and continue basting every 20-30 minutes until thermometer registers 170°.
- Remove from grill, let sit for 10 minutes, and slice. Serve with remaining sauce.
  Serves 4-6.

Best Pork Tenderloin

Simple, but super!

pork tenderloin
ground pepper

rosemary leaves

- Rinse tenderloin and rub with pepper and rosemary.
- Bake at 350° for 1 to 1½ hours depending on size of tenderloin. Meat thermometer should register 170°.
- Serve with barbeque sauce or chutney.
  Serves 3-4.

Luau Pork Tenderloin

Great with pasta or Hawaiian Beans.

½ cup honey
2 teaspoons prepared mustard
¼ cup brown sugar

2 tablespoons vinegar
¼ cup soy sauce
2 pork tenderloins

- Mix all the ingredients in shallow pan.
- Roll pork tenderloins in the mixture.
- Marinate 2-4 hours turning once or twice.
- Roast 1½ hours at 325°, or 1 hour at 350°.
- Baste frequently.
- Slice thin diagonal slices.
  Serves 4-6.

Chinese Pork Tenderloins

Duck Sauce:

2 tablespoons white vinegar
2 tablespoons sugar
2½ cups plum jelly or
  preserves

¼ teaspoon fresh ground
  ginger
1 cup Major Gray's Chutney,
  finely chopped

Mustard Sauce:

¼ cup dry mustard
1 teaspoon vinegar

water to make smooth paste

Pork Tenderloins:

2-4 whole pork tenderloins
3 garlic cloves, crushed
10 tablespoons sugar
4 teaspoons dark molasses
1 cup soy sauce

1 teaspoon salt
2 teaspoons hot mustard
4 tablespoons Duck Sauce
  (above)

Duck Sauce:
• Mix all ingredients until smooth.
Mustard Sauce:
• Add enough water to make a smooth paste.
Pork Tenderloins:
• Mix ingredients together and pour over pork tenderloins.
• Marinate in refrigerator 3-4 hours, or overnight.
• Bake 300° for 1 hour, longer for larger tenderloins. Baste with
  marinade.
• Slice thin and serve with Duck and Mustard sauces.
  Serves 6-8.

Spicy Baby Backs

6 pounds baby back ribs

Marinade:

1 tablespoon salt
1 tablespoon coarsely ground
  black pepper

2 teaspoons crushed red
  pepper flakes

Sauce:

1 cup cider vinegar
½ cup butter (not margarine)
4 tablespoons brown sugar

1 teaspoon crushed red pepper
  flakes

- Combine the marinade ingredients and rub all over the ribs. Let stand at least one hour.
- Combine the sauce ingredients in a sauce pan and bring to a boil. Simmer about 5 minutes. Set sauce aside and keep warm (or reheat as needed).
- Preheat oven to 400°. Place the ribs on a foil lined baking pan and brown in the oven for 15 minutes, turning once.
- Reduce the oven temperature to 350°. Baste the ribs with the sauce and continue baking the ribs for 2 hours in the 350° oven, turning and basting with warm sauce every 15 minutes.

Serves 6.

Waikiki Ribs

*4-5 pounds baby back loin pork
  ribs*

Marinade:

1 cup soy sauce
1 cup honey
1 cup ketchup
*3 tablespoons grated fresh
  ginger root*

2 cloves minced garlic
*½ teaspoon freshly ground
  pepper*
extra honey to glaze

- Parboil ribs for 30 minutes.
- Cut ribs individually and rub with seasoned salt.
- Mix marinade ingredients together.
- Combine ribs and marinade in a covered container. Refrigerate overnight.
- Glaze with honey, and bake in single layer on broiler pan at 350° for 30 minutes or until tender.
  Serves 4-6.

This can also be served as an appetizer.

Seafood

Swordfish Steaks with Three Sauces

6 swordfish steaks, 1" thick   1 cup dry white wine

Basil Mustard Butter:
1 stick sweet butter   ¼ cup chopped fresh basil
¼ cup Dijon mustard   leaves

Dill Butter:
1 stick sweet butter   ½ teaspoon lemon juice
3 tablespoons fresh dill,   ½ teaspoon Dijon mustard
   chopped

Curry Chutney Butter:
1 stick sweet butter   1 teaspoon curry powder
¼ cup mango chutney

- Preheat oven to 375°.
- Arrange swordfish steaks in single layer in 1 or 2 baking dishes.
- Pour wine around fish. Season with pepper.
- Bake in middle of oven for 10 minutes.
- Serve with flavored butters.
Butters:
- Mix ingredients together with melted butter.
   Serves 6.

Halibut with Tomato and Leek Sauce

2 leeks, rinsed and chopped   ¼ cup dry white wine
3 shallots, minced   2 tablespoons lemon juice
3 cloves garlic, minced   6 halibut steaks (6 ounces
1 tablespoon oil   each)
2 tomatoes, peeled, seeded and
   chopped

- Combine and cook leeks, shallots, garlic, tomatoes, wine, and
   lemon juice until the leeks are soft.
- Place fish in a 9x13 baking dish. Spoon sauce over top.
- Bake at 350° for 25 minutes or until fish flakes easily.
   Serves 6.

Red Snapper Vera Cruz

1 onion, chopped
4 shallots, minced
2 cloves garlic, minced
1 carrot, grated
1 tablespoon olive oil
1 can (14 ounces) stewed
  tomatoes, drained and
  chopped

1 can (4 ounces) diced green
  chilies
3 tablespoons lemon juice
2 tablespoons cilantro, chopped
cayenne pepper to taste
salt and pepper to taste
2 pounds red snapper

Great served with hot tortillas.

- Sauté onion, shallots, garlic, and carrots in olive oil until the onion is soft.
- Add tomatoes, chilies, lemon juice, and cilantro. Simmer for 5 minutes. Salt and pepper to taste.
- Place fish in a 9x13 baking dish. Pour sauce over the top. Bake at 350° for 20 minutes or until fish flakes easily and is opaque.
- Broil briefly to brown the vegetables.
Serves 6-8.

Ahi with Sesame-Cilantro Marinade

2 tablespoons sesame seeds
1 bunch scallions, thinly sliced
1 cup fresh cilantro, chopped
2 cloves garlic, crushed
¼ cup sesame oil

¼ cup honey
½ cup soy sauce
1 teaspoon Tabasco sauce
3 pounds Ahi tuna

Marinade is also terrific over swordfish or poultry.

Use 1 teaspoon crushed coriander seeds in place of fresh cilantro.

- Toast sesame seeds in a dry skillet over medium heat until golden. Set aside.
- Toss scallions, cilantro and garlic together.
- Add sesame seeds, sesame oil, honey, soy sauce, and Tabasco. Mix well. Keep refrigerated until ready to marinate.
- Pour over ahi in flat dish, cover with plastic wrap, and refrigerate 4-8 hours, turning occasionally.
- Cook on grill or broiler 4-7 minutes per side.
Serves 6.

Orange Roughy Cajun Style

¾ - 1 pound orange roughy
1 green pepper, sliced
1 red pepper, sliced
½ red onion, sliced

½-1 tablespoon margarine,
  melted
1 tablespoon Paul Prudhomme
  Seafood Seasoning

- Place fish on foil on cookie sheet. Brush fish with ½ of the margarine. Sprinkle with ½ of the seasoning.
- Cover fish with green pepper, red pepper, and red onion slices.
- Drizzle remaining margarine and sprinkle remaining seasoning on top of vegetables.
- Seal foil tightly. Bake on a barbecue grill or in the oven for 20 minutes at 350°.
  Serves 4.

Salmon with Capellini

1 pound capellini (angel hair
  pasta)
12 ounces fresh salmon-diced
1 cup sliced mushrooms
½ cup leeks
1 fresh tomato-diced

½ teaspoon fresh basil
2 cloves garlic-chopped
4 tablespoons olive oil
2-3 tablespoons flour
splash white wine

- Flour salmon and sauté in oil for one minute on each side.
- Add leeks for one minute.
- Add mushrooms.
- Drain off oil, and add a splash of wine.
- Add tomatoes, garlic, and basil.
- Reduce mixture.
- Cook pasta al dente and mix with sauce.
  Serves 4.

Broiled Salmon with Basil Mustard Sauce

4 salmon steaks, 6 ounces each
½ lemon, thinly sliced
1 stick butter
6 tablespoons Dijon mustard

2 tablespoons fresh basil,
* minced*
2 tablespoons olive oil
salt and pepper

- Preheat broiler. Place salmon in broiling pan sprayed with PAM.
- Brush ½ tablespoon olive oil on each steak. Salt and pepper. Add lemon slices on top.
- Broil until steaks are crusty on the outside, flaky and opaque inside.
- Melt butter in saucepan. Add mustard and basil and whisk together.
- Serve salmon steaks topped with sauce, or pass separately.
  Serves 4.

Shrimp with Lemon Rice

1 cup uncooked white rice
2 teaspoons ground tumeric
1 teaspoon mustard seeds
½ cup butter or margarine

2½ pounds raw shrimp, shelled
* and deveined*
1 teaspoon salt
1 cup dry white wine
2 tablespoons lemon juice

- Cook rice as directed.
- Sauté tumeric and mustard seeds in butter for 2-3 minutes.
- Stir in shrimp. Sauté for 5 minutes.
- Remove with slotted spoon and place in baking dish in refrigerator.
- Stir rice into drippings and heat until golden, stirring constantly. Add salt.
- Mix wine and lemon juice together and stir into rice mixture. Stir rice into shrimp. Cover and chill.
- Bake covered in 350° oven for 1 hour and 15 minutes. Fluff with fork before serving.
  Serves 8-10.

Malay Shrimp Satay

Shrimp cook great threaded onto skewers.

4 tablespoons green onions-sliced
4 gloves garlic-minced
4 tablespoons oil
1½ cups chicken broth
6 tablespoons peanut butter
2 tablespoons soy sauce
1 teaspoon finely grated lemon peel

½ teaspoon cayenne pepper
2 tablespoons lemon juice
2 teaspoons chili powder
1 teaspoon brown sugar
½ teaspoon ground ginger
1 pound shrimp-shelled, deveined, and with tails intact

- Sauté onion and garlic in oil until tender, but not brown.
- Add remaining ingredients EXCEPT shrimp.
- Simmer uncovered 10 minutes stirring frequently.
- Remove from heat and cool.
- Skim off any fat that rises to surface.
- Marinate shrimp in ½ of cooled mixture for one hour, turning to coat well.
- Remove shrimp from marinade and grill or broil. Shrimp should turn pink. Approximately 5-6 minutes per side.
- Serve peanut marinade on side.
  Serves 8.

Shrimp and Pepper Tortilla Crisps

16 tortillas (6"), flour or corn
½ cup vegetable oil
½ cup butter-melted
¼ pound Monterey Jack
  cheese, grated
¼ pound Cheddar cheese,
  grated
16 fresh jumbo shrimp,
  cleaned, tails intact

½ cup olive oil
1 large red bell pepper-
  julienned
1 large yellow bell pepper-
  julienned
2 green bell peppers-julienned
3 cloves garlic-minced

- Preheat oven to 400°.
- Soak tortillas in mixture of vegetable oil and melted butter for about 30 minutes.
- Place tortillas on several rimmed baking sheets and bake in 400° oven for about 10 minutes or until crisp.
- Remove tortillas from oven, top with mixture of cheese. Bake again until cheese melts. Remove from oven.
- Heat olive oil in a large skillet. Add minced garlic and julienned peppers to oil. Sauté over medium-high heat for about 2 minutes.
- Add the shrimp and cook for about 3-4 minutes longer until shrimp are just cooked through. Remove from heat.
- Top each tortilla crisp with shrimp and pepper mixture. Serve while still warm.
  Serves 16.

Also wonderful as an appetizer. Beautiful colors.

Crab Casserole

*Can be prepared
a day before and
refrigerated.*

½ pound lasagna noodles
1 tablespoon oil
2 cans (10.5 ounces) cream of
   shrimp soup
1 pound crabmeat
2 cups small curd cottage
   cheese
1 package (8 ounces) cream
   cheese

1 egg, slightly beaten
1 mild onion, chopped
2 teaspoons basil
½ teaspoon lemon juice
salt and pepper to taste
2 tomatoes, thinly sliced
shredded Cheddar cheese

- Cook noodles in salted water with oil for 15 minutes. Drain and rinse in cold water.
- Combine soup and crab in separate bowl. Mix in cottage cheese, cream cheese, egg, onion, basil, lemon juice, salt and pepper.
- In a large shallow buttered casserole dish, place one layer of noodles, half cheese mixture, and all the crab mixture.
- Cover with another layer of noodles and remaining cheese. Top with layer of tomatoes.
- Bake 15 minutes at 350°. Add a layer of Cheddar cheese and return to oven for 30 minutes or until brown and bubbly. Let stand several minutes before cutting in squares.
  Serves 8-12.

Crab Spinach Fettuccini

1 tablespoon butter
½ pound imitation crab
8 ounces spinach fettuccini

Contadina Pesto Sauce (7
   ounces)
½ cup whipping cream
½ cup Parmesan cheese

- Sauté crab in butter. Add pesto.
- Add whipping cream and cook until warm.
- Cook noodles to desired consistency. Drain.
- Pour sauce over noodles.
- Add ½ cup Parmesan cheese and toss.
  Serves 4.

Crab Mousse with Cucumber Sauce

8 ounces crab meat (or 8 ounces canned)
1 cup celery, minced
4 hard boiled eggs, chopped
2 tablespoons sweet pickle relish

1 small onion, minced
1 small green pepper, minced
1 cup mayonnaise
1 envelope Knox gelatin

Cucumber Sauce:
½ cup sour cream
⅛ teaspoon salt
⅛ teaspoon pepper

3 tablespoons lemon juice
1 cucumber, chopped

- Add gelatin to ¼ cup cold water and then dissolve in ¼ cup hot water.
- Mix crab, celery, eggs, relish, onion, pepper, mayonnaise, and gelatin together.
- Put in individual molds or one large mold.
- Refrigerate at least 6 hours.

Cucumber Sauce:
- Beat sour cream until stiff.
- Add salt, pepper, and lemon juice.
- Add cucumber last.
- Serve on top of mold slices.
  Serves 6-8.

Wonderful as an entree for lunch, or as an appetizer.

Accompaniments

Sun Kissed Carrots

6-8 large sweet carrots
2 tablespoons sweet unsalted
  butter
juice of 1 orange
orange rind

¼ cup brown sugar
¼ teaspoon nutmeg
⅛ teaspoon cinnamon
dash of salt

- Cook or steam carrots until tender.
- Place carrots and all ingredients in blender and blend until smooth.
- Put in a soufflé dish and sprinkle with additional nutmeg and orange rind for color.
- Bake at 350° for 20-30 minutes.
  Serves 4-6.

Carrot Timbales

*May make this in
one large mold,
but increase
cooking time.*

2 pounds carrots
2 tablespoons butter or
  margarine
1 teaspoon sugar
1 teaspoon salt

¼ teaspoon pepper
1 small onion, chopped
3 eggs, beaten
½ cup cream
½ cup half and half

- Cook carrots with 2 tablespoons butter and sugar until soft. (Add small amount of water to help cook.) Mash.
- Add remaining ingredients.
- Pour into a ring or individual molds sprayed with Pam. Place them in a pan of water.
- Bake 40 minutes at 350° or until it leaves the sides of the mold.
  Serves 6-8.

Curried Carrots

1¼ pound carrots, peeled,
  halved lengthwise, and sliced
  diagonally into ½" slices
1 tablespoon honey
½ tablespoon fresh lemon juice
1 teaspoon Dijon mustard

1½ teaspoons curry powder
2 tablespoons safflower oil
½ tablespoon unsalted butter
  or margarine
½ tablespoon brown sugar
⅓ cup raisins

- Steam carrots for 10 minutes. Remove from heat and uncover.
- Combine the honey, lemon juice, mustard and curry powder.
- Sauté carrots for 2 minutes in oil and butter over medium-high heat.
- Sprinkle brown sugar over carrots, add raisins and cook for 2 more minutes, stirring constantly.
- Stir in the honey mixture and cook for 3 more minutes. Serve immediately.
Serves 4-6.

Orange Walnut Broccoli

1½ pounds broccoli, cut into
  serving size spears
2 packages (3 ounces) cream
  cheese
¼ cup milk
½ teaspoon salt

½ teaspoon grated orange peel
¼ teaspoon thyme leaves
¼ cup orange juice
3 tablespoons walnuts,
  chopped

- Cook broccoli in boiling water until crisp-tender, about 10-12 minutes. Drain and keep warm in a serving dish.
- Cook cream cheese, milk, salt, orange peel, orange juice, and thyme over medium heat until smooth, stirring occasionally.
- Pour orange sauce over broccoli and sprinkle with nuts. Garnish with orange slices.
Serves 6.

Joanne Menapace, Chef
Cathy's Rum Cake Caterers

Elegant Broccoli

1¼ pounds fresh broccoli
2 tablespoons butter
1 tablespoon lemon juice
2 egg whites
⅓ cup mayonnaise

2 tablespoons Parmesan
  cheese, grated
paprika
lemon wedges

- Cook broccoli until tender.
- Melt butter in saucepan, remove from heat, and add lemon juice. Keep warm.
- Beat egg whites until stiff and fold in mayonnaise with rubber spatula.
- Drain broccoli, arrange in oblong glass 1½-2 quart casserole with stem ends towards center.
- Pour lemon-butter sauce over flower end of broccoli.
- Spoon egg white mixture down the center covering the stem ends.
- Sprinkle grated cheese and paprika on top.
- Broil on middle rack until topping is puffy and golden brown.
- Garnish with lemon wedges and serve immediately.
  Serves 6-8.

Cheese-stuffed Brocciflower

Refrigerate any leftovers immediately. Cut into pieces and place in a tossed salad the next day.

1 large head brocciflower, trimmed and left whole
6 ounces Cheddar cheese, cut in strips
salt and pepper to taste

¼ cup melted butter or margarine
½ cup herb stuffing
½ cup Parmesan cheese

- Cook brocciflower in boiling salted water until tender but still firm. Drain.
- Place in shallow baking dish.
- Press strips of cheese into brocciflower all over the head.
- Sprinkle with salt and pepper.
- Pour melted butter over top.
- Sprinkle with Parmesan cheese and bread crumbs.
- Bake in 350° oven for 20 minutes. Could be broiled for last 2-3 minutes to brown top.
  Serves 6-8.

Onion Quiche

1 cup Saltine crackers, crushed
1 cup butter
½ teaspoon dry mustard
4 eggs, beaten

¾ cup milk
3 medium onions cut in rings
1 cup grated Cheddar cheese

- Mix ½ cup melted butter with crushed saltines. Pat in bottom of pie pan sprayed with Pam.
- Sauté onions in ½ cup butter until lightly yellow. Place on top of saltine crust.
- Mix eggs, mustard, and milk together. Pour over onions.
- Top with grated cheese.
- Bake at 350° for 35 minutes or until set.
  Serves 6-8.

Great side dish served with grilled steak, or for lunch with a green salad.

May add fresh broccoli or zucchini for additional color.

Eggplant Ramekins

3 small eggplants, unpeeled
¾ pound mushrooms, sliced
¼ cup onion, minced
3 tablespoons fresh parsley, minced
3 large tomatoes, seeded, drained and chopped

1 teaspoon dried oregano
2 teaspoons dried basil
1 teaspoon dried thyme
3 tablespoons olive oil
¼ cup Romano cheese, grated
parsley sprigs to garnish

- Bake eggplants for 30 minutes in 375° oven. Do not turn off oven.
- Run eggplants under cold water to cool. Scoop out and chop insides.
- Mix with all other ingredients EXCEPT oil, Romano cheese, and parsley.
- Sauté mixture for 5 minutes in olive oil. Fill ramekins with mixture and top with Romano cheese.
- Bake 10 minutes. Broil until top is brown.
  Serves 6.

You could also fill the eggplant halves.

Spaghetti Squash Marinara

2 teaspoons olive oil
2 teaspoons margarine
1-2 cloves garlic, minced
¾ cup chopped onions
1 can (4 ounces) sliced
  mushrooms, drained
1 can (14.5 ounces) Italian
  style stewed tomatoes

1 tablespoon chopped parsley
½ teaspoon dried basil
¾ cup grated fresh Parmesan
  cheese
½ large spaghetti squash
salt and pepper to taste

- Heat olive oil and margarine in a large non-stick pan.
- Sauté garlic and onions for 5 minutes.
- Add mushrooms and sauté 2 minutes.
- Add canned tomatoes, parsley, and basil. Cover and simmer 15 minutes.
- While sauce is simmering, cut squash in half length wise and remove seeds.
- Place squash in ⅓ cup of water in pyrex dish, cut side down. Cover with plastic wrap and microwave on high for 10 minutes.
- Scoop out spaghetti strands into serving dish. Top with simmered sauce and Parmesan cheese.
Serves 4-6.

Orange Glazed "Hot" Green Beans

Be careful while handling Serrano chilies. Be sure to wash hands thoroughly after handling and keep hands away from your face.

4 Serrano chilies, stems and
  seeds removed, cut in thin
  strips
1 pound French cut green
  beans, frozen or canned

2 tablespoons orange juice
2 teaspoons orange zest or
  grated orange peel
¼ cup butter, melted
¼ cup light brown sugar

- Marinate the chilies, green beans, orange juice and zest for 1 hour.
- Add sugar to melted butter until it dissolves.
- Add the green bean mixture and simmer until the beans are glazed and cooked.
Serves 4.

Joanne Menapace, Chef
Cathy's Rum Cake Caterers

Herbed Asparagus with Parmesan Cheese

*2 pounds pencil thin
asparagus, trimmed*

*4 tablespoons unsalted butter,
softened*

*1 tablespoon fresh Italian
parsley, chopped*

*1 tablespoon fresh or freeze-
dried chives*

*1 tablespoon fresh dill,
chopped*

*1 tablespoon fresh rosemary,
chopped*

*1 teaspoon coarsely ground
black pepper*

*4 ounces Parmesan cheese,
grated*

- Cook asparagus until tender, 1½ to 2 minutes in boiling water. Drain and pat dry.
- Blend butter, herbs and pepper.
- Melt herbed butter over medium heat just before serving. Add asparagus and toss gently to heat through, about 2 minutes.
- Place on serving platter and sprinkle Parmesan cheese over top.
  Serves 6.

Joanne Menapace, Chef
Cathy's Rum Cake Caterers

Picante Corn Casserole

1 stick margarine

*1 package (8 ounces) cream
cheese*

*12 ounces frozen white corn,
thawed and drained*

3 tablespoons onion, chopped

*1 can (4 ounces) diced green
chilies*

salt to taste

2 tablespoons hot salsa

*This tastes great
with BBQ.*

*Try adding onions
or pimentos for
added flavor.*

- Melt margarine over low heat. Add cream cheese and stir until melted.
- Combine remaining ingredients and add to cream cheese mixture.
- Bake, uncovered, 35 minutes at 350° in a 2 quart casserole.
- May be made ahead and refrigerated.
  Serves 8.

Chile Rellenos Casserole

1 cup half and half
2 eggs
⅓ cup flour
3 cans (4 ounces) whole green
  chilies

½ pound Monterey Jack cheese,
  grated
½ pound sharp Cheddar
  cheese, grated
1 can (8 ounces) tomato sauce

- Beat half and half with eggs and flour until smooth.
- Split chilies, rinse out seeds and drain.
- Mix cheeses, reserving ½ cup for topping.
- Make alternate layers of cheese, chilies, and egg mixture in deep 1½ quart casserole dish.
- Pour tomato sauce over top and sprinkle with reserved cheese.
- Bake in 375° oven for 1 hour, until cooked in center.
  Serves 4.

Hawaiian Beans

Great with chicken or pork.

½ pound diced bacon, browned
1 diced onion
½ cup ketchup
1 teaspoon salt
1 can (15.5 ounces) butter
  beans
1 can (15 ounces) kidney beans
1 can (16 ounces) pork &
  beans

1 can (15 ounces) pinto beans
1 can (17 ounces) lima beans
¾ cup brown sugar
2 teaspoons mustard
¼ cup pineapple juice
1 teaspoon vinegar
1 tablespoon BBQ sauce

- Drain beans, and mix all ingredients together.
- Bake 1 hour at 350° or cook in a crock pot on low for 7 hours.
  Serves 10-12.

Potatoes au Beurre

6-8 medium baking potatoes,
  peeled
2-3 teaspoons salt
⅛ teaspoon pepper
3 tablespoons fresh parsley,
  minced

1 cup sharp Cheddar cheese,
  grated
6 tablespoons butter
1 cup whipping cream
2 tablespoons fresh minced
  parsley for top

Easy and elegant.

- Cut potatoes into ½ inch thick strips, resembling french fries.
- Layer into a 9 x 13 baking dish. Sprinkle with salt, pepper, 3 tablespoons parsley, and cheese.
- Dot with butter and pour cream over. Sprinkle with 2 tablespoons parsley.
- Bake in 350° oven for 1½ - 2 hours, covered.
- Remove cover last half hour to brown.
  Serves 6-8.

Rondele Potatoes

2 cups whipping cream
1 package (4 ounces) Rondele
  cheese with herbs

3 pounds red new potatoes,
  unpeeled, scrubbed, thinly
  sliced
1½ tablespoons chopped fresh
  parsley

*Try using your
favorite cheeses
and herbs.*

- Preheat oven to 400°.
- Butter 9 x 13 baking dish.
- Mix cheese and cream together over medium heat until mixture is smooth.
- Arrange half of potatoes in baking dish in overlapping rows. Generously season with salt and pepper.
- Pour half of cheese mixture over top.
- Repeat with potatoes and cheese mixture.
- Bake until top is golden brown and potatoes are tender when pierced with knife, about 1 hour.
- Sprinkle with fresh parsley.
  Serves 6-8.

Crab Potato Bake

9 ounces crab meat, shredded
⅔ cup Cheddar cheese, grated
4 baking potatoes
⅓ cup butter, melted

½ cup sour cream
⅓ cup green onion, diced
salt and pepper to taste

- Bake four potatoes, cut in half and scoop out insides.
- Mix all ingredients with cooked potatoes. (Set aside small amount of cheese to sprinkle on top.) Restuff in potato jackets.
- Bake in baking dish at 350° for 20-30 minutes.
  Serves 8.

Four Cheese Potatoes

Great with steaks, ribs, etc.

12 medium red potatoes, unpeeled, cut into 1 inch cubes
8 ounces Mozzarella cheese, grated
⅓ cup Parmesan cheese
2 cups ricotta cheese
1 cup sour cream

3 cups Cheddar cheese, grated
¼ cup green onions, finely chopped
3 tablespoons parsley, chopped
1 teaspoon basil
¼ teaspoon pepper
2 cloves garlic, crushed

- Cook cubed potatoes in boiling water for approximately 10 minutes, until barely tender. Drain.
- In a large bowl mix remaining ingredients together, reserving 1½ cups Cheddar cheese for topping.
- Carefully mix in the potatoes. Spoon mixture into greased 9 x 13 casserole.
- Sprinkle with Cheddar cheese.
- Bake 30 minutes at 350°.
  Serves 8-10.

Roasted New Potatoes

2 pounds red new potatoes
3 small onions, cut in quarters
¼ cup melted butter

½ teaspoon salt
½ teaspoon marjoram leaves
¼ teaspoon pepper

- Melt butter and add to a 2 quart casserole. Stir in marjoram, salt and pepper.
- Turn potatoes in melted mixture to coat.
- Cover dish and bake in a 400° oven for 1 to 1½ hours.
- Turn once during cooking.
  Serves 8-10.

Crunchy Caramel Sweet Potato Balls

3 medium sweet potatoes,
  peeled and quartered
1½ teaspoons cinnamon
⅛ teaspoon allspice
¼ cup Grand Marnier
2 cups Grape Nuts

1 tablespoon diet margarine or
  butter
½ cup brown sugar, packed
  tightly
3 tablespoons light corn syrup
½ teaspoon nutmeg

- Place sweet potato pieces in a 1½ quart casserole. Cover. Microwave for 6 minutes on high. Remove and stir. Microwave for an additional 6 minutes.
- Mash potatoes. Stir in cinnamon, allspice and Grand Marnier until smooth.
- Shape mixture into 2" balls. Roll each ball in Grape Nuts. Arrange in a 12x7 baking dish.
- Melt margarine in a small saucepan. Add brown sugar, corn syrup and nutmeg. Stir until smooth and bubbly. Pour over balls.
- Microwave for 5 minutes on high. Let stand for several minutes before serving.
  Serves 4.

Rice Pecan Casserole

1 pound mushrooms, sliced
4 green onions, sliced
1 clove garlic, minced
1 cup unsalted sweet butter
2 cups uncooked brown rice
½ teaspoon dried thyme leaves
¼ teaspoon turmeric
1 teaspoon salt

¼ teaspoon freshly ground pepper
1½ cups chopped pecans
6 cups beef stock or 3 cans (10¾ ounces) condensed beef broth diluted with 2¼ cups water

- Sauté mushrooms, garlic, and onions in butter in large Dutch oven until onions are golden, about 5-7 minutes.
- Stir in rice, cook, stirring with fork until rice is hot, about 3 minutes.
- Add thyme, turmeric, salt and pepper.
- Add chopped pecans.
- Pour in stock and heat to boiling.
- Bake covered at 400° for 1 hour 20 minutes until liquid is absorbed and rice is tender.
Serves 10-12.

Mushroom Barley Casserole

⅓ cup butter
⅔ cup onion, chopped
⅔ cup celery, sliced
1 cup Pearled Barley

1 can (10 ounces) cream of mushroom soup
2 cups water
¼ cup fresh parsley or 2 tablespoons dried flakes

- Preheat oven to 350°. Grease 8" square baking dish.
- Sauté onion and celery in butter until tender. Add barley and cook 2 minutes or until light golden brown, stirring frequently.
- Combine remaining ingredients in a bowl. Add barley mixture and mix well.
- Pour into baking dish, cover and cook 1 hour and 15 minutes or until liquid is absorbed. Stir before serving.
Serves 6-8.

Cranberry Walnut Relish

16 ounces fresh cranberries
1½ cups sugar
3 tablespoons fresh lemon or
   lime juice

1 cup orange marmalade
1 cup walnuts, coarsely
   chopped

- Wash and drain cranberries. Mix with sugar and spread on jelly roll pan lined with foil. Bake in 350° oven for 1 hour.
- Spread walnuts on baking sheet and toast in oven for 10 minutes.
- Mix orange marmalade with lemon juice. Add cranberries and nuts. Mix and chill, covered for at least 6 hours.
  Makes 2 cups.

Brandied Cranberries

1 pound (12 ounces bag is fine)
   fresh cranberries

2 cups light brown sugar
¼ cup brandy

- Sprinkle sugar over cranberries in a heavy oven-proof skillet. Cover and place in 250° oven for 1 hour.
- Remove and pour in brandy. Recover skillet for 5 minutes.
- Serve warm.
  Serves 6.

Great for Thanksgiving and so easy! The cranberries "pop" in your mouth.

Pasta

Seafood with Spinach Pasta

*1 package (12 ounces) spinach
 fettuccini*
2 cups heavy cream
*1 cup (½ pound) fresh salmon,
 diced*
1 cup (½ pound) scallops

1 red pepper, julienned
*¾ cup fresh snow peas, ends
 trimmed*
*⅔ cup fresh Parmesan cheese,
 grated*

- Cook pasta until al dente.
- Bring cream to a gentle boil and reduce to 1½ cups.
- Add fish and vegetables to cream cooking gently for 5 minutes.
- Remove from heat and add cheese. (The sauce will be thin.)
- Toss pasta and sauce together. Sprinkle with more Parmesan cheese.
  Serves 4-6.

Pasta with Scallops and Lemony Mustard Sauce

5 ounces dry angel hair pasta
1 tablespoon butter
*1 tablespoon fresh chives,
 chopped*
1 cup white wine
½ pound small bay scallops

½ teaspoon lemon peel, grated
2 teaspoons Dijon mustard
*4 tablespoons butter, cut into 4
 pieces*
salt and pepper to taste

- Simmer wine and lemon peel in medium skillet. Add scallops and sauté until almost opaque. Remove scallops with slotted spoon to separate bowl.
- Increase skillet heat and boil, reducing sauce to ¼ cup (about 6 minutes).
- Reduce heat to low and whisk in mustard. Add butter one piece at a time, whisking continuously.
- Add scallops and remaining juices, heating through. Salt and pepper to taste.
- Cook pasta in boiling salted water until al dente. Drain and toss with 1 tablespoon butter.
- Divide pasta between 2 plates and spoon scallops over. Sprinkle with chives.
  Serves 2.

Spinach Pasta with Fresh Tomato Vinaigrette

*1 package (12 ounces) spinach
  pasta
3 large ripe tomatoes (2 cups),
  peeled, seeded and chopped.
½ cup chopped fresh herbs—
  such as basil, tarragon,
  thyme, oregano, parsley, etc.*

*⅓ cup garlic red wine vinegar
4 large shallots, chopped
⅓ cup extra virgin olive oil
Parmesan cheese, grated*

*Try topping with
chunks of fresh
broiled salmon.*

- Mix tomatoes, herbs, vinegar, shallots, and oil together.
- Cook pasta al-dente and drain.
- Toss sauce and pasta, and garnish with herb sprigs and fresh grated Parmesan.
- Best served at room temperature.
  Serves 6.

Pasta with Fresh Lemon Dill Sauce

*1 package (12 ounces)
  fettuccini
6 ounces unsalted butter
1 cup heavy cream
juice and grated peel of 1 large
  lemon*

*2 teaspoons fresh dill, chopped
fresh ground white pepper to
  taste
fresh ground nutmeg, a pinch
½ cup fresh Parmesan, grated*

*Can use as a side
dish or main
course.*

- Cook pasta al-dente, drain.
- Melt butter in large skillet over low flame.
- Add cooked pasta to melted butter.
- Add cream, lemon peel, juice, dill, white pepper, salt and nutmeg.
- Mix and reduce one to two minutes over medium to high heat.
- Garnish with parsley sprigs and Parmesan.
  Serves 4 as a main dish.

Four Cheese Fettuccini

¼ cup margarine or butter
½ cup half & half
½ cup Gruyère cheese,
  shredded
¼ cup Parmesan cheese,
  grated
½ teaspoon salt
⅛ teaspoon ground pepper

1 clove garlic, finely chopped
8 ounces uncooked fettuccini
2 tablespoons olive oil
½ cup Sweet Gorganzola
  cheese, grated
½ cup Mozzarella cheese,
  shredded
1 teaspoon snipped parsley

- Melt margarine in 2 quart saucepan over low heat.
- Sauté garlic, and add half & half.
- Stir in Gruyère, Parmesan, salt, and pepper.
- Cook, stirring occasionally, for 5 minutes.
- Cook fettuccini as directed adding oil to boiling water.
- Drain fettuccini and add to sauce.
- Add Gorganzola and Mozzarella cheese.
- Toss and sprinkle with parsley.
  Serves 4.

Pasta Asiago

*Add some
chopped tomatoes
for color.*

½ package linguine
½ cup virgin olive oil
1 cup frozen green peas,
  thawed
1 medium zucchini, quartered
  and sliced diagonally into
  ⅛" strips

⅓ pound snow peas, trimmed
1⅓ cups Asiago cheese, grated
⅓ cup parsley, chopped
1 teaspoon white pepper
½ teaspoon salt
1 tablespoon fresh garlic,
  minced

- Cook linguine al dente. Drain and rinse under cold water. Shake out excess water.
- Put linguine in large bowl and toss in the olive oil.
- Add remaining ingredients and toss well.
- Let sit a couple of hours before serving. Serve chilled, but not ice cold.
  Serves 9-12.

Thank you to Linda Bosse of Slight Indulgence.

Noodle Pudding

½ pound wide noodles
1 pound cottage cheese
1 pint sour cream
¼ cup milk
½ cup margarine or butter,
  melted

¼ cup sugar
½ cup raisins
5-6 eggs
1 teaspoon vanilla

Topping:
2½ cups cornflakes
¼ pound margarine, melted

1 cup brown sugar

- Cook noodles al-dente and drain.
- Beat eggs with sugar, adding noodles and remaining ingredients.
- Pour in buttered oblong pan.
- Mix together topping ingredients and spread over top of noodles.
- Bake 40-50 minutes at 300°.
  Serves 6-8.

Makes a wonderful side dish.

Can use frosted flakes to sprinkle on top, without the margarine and brown sugar.

Lasagna Rolls

8 lasagna noodles, cooked

Filling:
2 packages (10 ounces each)
  frozen chopped broccoli
  (thawed and drained)
1 cup Parmesan cheese, grated
1 cup Italian bread crumbs

½ cup dried onion flakes
1 can (6 ounces) tomato paste
2 egg whites
2 teaspoons garlic powder
2 teaspoons Italian seasoning

Topping:
3 cups spaghetti sauce

12 ounces low fat Mozzarella
  cheese, shredded

A great vegetarian dish.

- Mix all the filling ingredients together.
- Spread 3 heaping tablespoons of filling on each noodle.
- Roll each noodle and place in pan side by side.
- Top with sauce and sprinkle with cheese.
- Bake 20 minutes at 325°.
  Serves 8.

Spinach Lasagna

Makes a great luncheon dish with a salad.

Can use sliced tomatoes in place of spinach.

1 package (10 ounces) lasagna noodles, cooked
2 packages (10 ounces each) frozen spinach, uncooked and well drained
1 pound Monterey Jack cheese, grated (reserve ½ cup)
1 cup Parmesan cheese, grated
2 pounds small curd cottage cheese
2 eggs
1 tablespoon parsley, chopped
½ cup butter or margarine, melted
garlic salt, salt and pepper to taste

- Mix cottage cheese, eggs, parsley, butter, salt, and pepper together.
- Add a little garlic salt to spinach.
- Grease 9 x 13 casserole, and put in a layer of noodles.
- Follow by a layer of cottage cheese mix, layer of Jack cheese, sprinkle with Parmesan, then a layer of spinach. Repeat.
- Finish with ½ cup of Parmesan cheese on top.
- Bake at 350° for 30 minutes or until bubbly.
  Serves 10-12.

Festive Chicken Fettuccini

1 cup chicken, cooked and cubed
1 cup fresh asparagus, cut into 1" pieces
½ cup fresh red bell pepper, diced
½ cup fresh mushrooms, sliced
6 ounces dry fettuccini
¼ cup butter or margarine, softened
½ cup whipping cream at room temperature
2 teaspoons crushed garlic
⅓ cup Parmesan cheese, grated
salt and pepper to taste

- Cook chicken and cube. Keep warm.
- Layer the asparagus, red pepper, and mushrooms (in that order) in a vegetable steamer. Steam until all the vegetables are tender. Remove from stove and keep warm.
- Cook fettuccini according to package directions. Drain and return to cooking pot.
- Add butter, whipping cream, Parmesan cheese, garlic, salt, and pepper to warm fettuccini. Toss and coat.
- Add chicken and vegetables to fettuccini. Toss again. Serve immediately.
  Serves 4.

Chinese Spaghetti

1 package (12 ounces)
  spaghetti
1 frying chicken, cut into pieces
2-4 tablespoons olive oil
½ cup green onions, chopped
1 cup green peppers, sliced
½ cup parsley, chopped
2 cups broccoli, chopped

1 cup celery, chopped
2 cups mushrooms, sliced
1 jar (3 ounces) Spanish olives,
  sliced
salt, pepper, and garlic powder
  to taste
1 cup Parmesan cheese, grated

- Fry chicken pieces in olive oil. Cool, skin, bone, and shred.
- Sauté all the vegetables in the chicken drippings until tender.
- Cook spaghetti according to package directions. Drain.
- Combine chicken, spaghetti and vegetables. Toss with salt, pepper, and garlic powder to taste.
- Toss with Parmesan cheese and serve immediately.
Serves 8-10.

Noodles Romanoff with Chicken

4 cups (8 halves) chicken
  breasts, cooked
1 package (8 ounces) wide egg
  noodles
1 can (10¾ ounces) cream of
  chicken soup
1 can (2 ounces) pimentos
¼ pound mushrooms, sliced
  and sautéed
3 ounces Parmesan cheese,
  grated

1 cup mayonnaise
½ cup sour cream
1 tablespoon minced onion
1 cup diced celery
1 can (8 ounces) water
  chestnuts
⅓ cup sauterne
dash cayenne
salt and pepper to taste

*Can be made
ahead and frozen-
uncooked.*

- Cook noodles al-dente.
- Mix all ingredients EXCEPT ½ cup mayonnaise together.
- In a 9 x 12 baking dish, layer noodles on bottom, chicken, and sauce. Repeat.
- Let stand overnight in refrigerator.
- Add remaining mayonnaise (½ cup) on top and additional Parmesan.
- Bake covered in 350° oven for 35 minutes. Uncover and bake an additional 10 minutes or until bubbly.
Serves 8-10.

Desserts

Frozen Chambord Torte with Raspberry Sauce

Crust:
2 cups crushed vanilla wafers (50 wafers)

1½ cups chopped slivered almonds

6 tablespoons unsalted butter, melted

2 tablespoons sugar

Filling:
6 large egg yolks

½ cup sugar

6 tablespoons Chambord liqueur

2½ cups whipping cream

6 tablespoons powdered sugar

1 tablespoon vanilla

Sauce:
1 bag (12 ounces) frozen raspberries

¼ cup sugar

1 tablespoon Chambord

Crust
- Butter a 9x2½" springform pan.
- Mix all ingredients in large bowl.
- Press mixture onto bottom and sides of pan.

Filling
- Blend yolks, sugar and liqueur in large bowl. Place over saucepan of boiling water.
- Whisk egg mixture until thick and creamy, about 4 minutes. Remove bowl from heat.
- Continue whisking until cool, about 5 minutes.
- Using an electric mixer, beat cream, powdered sugar and vanilla in another large bowl until stiff peaks form.
- Fold cream mixture into egg mixture. Pour filling into crust and freeze overnight. Cover with plastic-good for 3 days in freezer.

Sauce
- Puree thawed raspberries, sugar and liqueur in blender until smooth. Strain. Can be prepared up to two days ahead, covered and refrigerated.
- Decorate top of torte with alternating rows of raspberries and sliced almonds. Swirl sauce on plate for design and place slice of torte on top. Spoon sauce on top and garnish with mint sprig. Let torte thaw 10 minutes before cutting.

Serves 12-16.

Apple and Caramel Cheese Tart

Crust:
1¼ cups flour
¼ cup sugar
½ teaspoon cinnamon
½ cup butter, softened

Filling:
1 package (8 ounces) cream cheese, softened
½ cup sugar
1 teaspoon favorite liqueur
1 tablespoon flour
1 egg, beaten

Topping:
⅓ cup pecans, chopped
3 Granny Smith or Pippin apples, peeled, cored, and sliced
¾ cup caramel ice cream topping
½ teaspoon cinnamon

Our favorite liqueur to use is amaretto or raspberry brandy. You can also substitute vanilla or almond extract.

Crust:
- Preheat oven to 375°.
- Combine flour, sugar, and cinnamon in medium bowl.
- Cut in butter until it resembles crumbs. Reserve ⅓ of mixture for top.
- Press remaining into bottom and sides of 11" tart pan.
- Pierce dough with fork and bake at 375° for 15 minutes. Set aside and prepare filling.

Filling:
- Beat cream cheese and liqueur until smooth.
- Beat in sugar and flour gradually and then the egg.
- Pour into hot crust. Bake about 15 minutes until filling is set.

Topping:
- Combine pecans and reserved crust mixture in small bowl.
- Combine apples, caramel and cinnamon in another bowl.
- Working quickly, arrange apples on top of filling. Spoon remaining caramel from bowl over top and sprinkle with pecan mixture.
- Bake until apples are tender, about 20-25 minutes.
- Cool on a wire rack.
  Serves 6-8.

Tart Au Citron

Pastry:

1¾ cups flour

¼ cup almonds, slivered

1 large egg

1 tablespoon milk

1 teaspoon almond extract

1½ sticks butter

1 tablespoon sugar, heaping

Filling:

1 cup sugar

1 stick unsalted butter

⅓ cup lemon juice and rinds

3 eggs

Pastry:

- Finely chop almonds in a food processor. Remove from bowl.
- Place egg, milk, almond extract and butter in bowl and process on and off.
- Add flour, sugar, and almonds and process until dough begins to mass together. Do not allow it to form a ball.
- Gather together and place in refrigerator to chill

Filling:

- Place sugar, butter, rind, and strained juice in a pan. Bring to a boil.
- Mix eggs in a separate bowl. Whisk hot butter mixture into the eggs.
- Return the entire mixture to pan. Cook slowly over low heat until the mixture is thick and coats the back of a spoon. DO NOT BOIL! Chill.
- Set oven at 375°.
- Take ⅔ of pastry and roll it ¼" thick to fit in a 9" flan pan. Prick the bottom and chill for 5 minutes. Fill with cold lemon filling.
- Roll out remaining pastry to fit the top of the tart. Seal the edges and mark the top with a spiral with the point of a knife.
- Bake 30 minutes. Remove and brush the top with a beaten egg white. Sprinkle with sugar.
- Return to oven and bake 10 minutes.
  Serves 12-14.

Chocolate Walnut Torte

4 ounces unsweetened
  chocolate
2 sticks butter
4 large eggs
2 cups sugar

1 cup unsifted flour
1 tablespoon Myers dark rum
2 teaspoons vanilla
¼ teaspoon salt
 2 cups walnut halves

This torte can be stored for 2-3 days at room temperature or frozen up to 2 months!

Icing:

1½ ounces unsweetened
  chocolate
1½ tablespoons butter, melted
1½ cups unsifted powdered
  sugar

1½ tablespoons dark rum
1 tablespoon water
12 perfect walnut halves

- Preheat oven to 350°.
- Grease 8" or 9" cake pan with shortening, and line pan with circle of greased parchment paper.
- Melt chocolate with butter over low heat in double boiler or in microwave on medium-high heat for 60-95 seconds. Set aside.
- Place eggs in large mixing bowl with sugar and beat with whisk until just blended and smooth. Do not over beat.
- Stir in the chocolate mixture and add flour, vanilla, salt and rum. Mix well.
- Fold in nuts and pour batter in pan.
- Bake for 40-45 minutes. Cool in pan 10 minutes, then turn out and remove parchment paper.
- Ice the cake while still warm.

Icing:
- Melt chocolate and butter as before.
- Blend in powdered sugar, rum and water. Add additional water for right consistency.
- Spread immediately over warm torte. Don't fuss with this icing as it will lose its gloss.
- Garnish with 12 walnut halves around the border.
  Serves 8-10.

Frozen Berry Chiffon

1 cup flour, unsifted
¼ cup firmly packed brown
* sugar*
½ cup pecans, chopped
½ cup butter or margarine
3 cups whole berries
* (raspberries, strawberries, or*
* blackberries)*

1 cup sugar
2 egg whites
2 teaspoons lemon juice
1 cup whipping cream

- In a bowl combine flour, brown sugar, and nuts.
- Cut butter in small pieces and rub into flour mixture with your fingers until crumbly.
- Sprinkle mixture on a rimmed baking sheet. Bake in a 375° oven for about 15 minutes or until golden brown. Stir frequently. Cool and set aside ½ cup.
- Spread remaining crumbs in the bottom of a 10" cheesecake pan with removable sides.
- In the large bowl of an electric mixer, combine 2 cups of the berries, sugar, egg whites and lemon juice.
- Beat on low speed to blend, then on high speed until firm peaks form, about 15 minutes.
- Whip cream in a separate bowl until very soft peaks form, then gently but thoroughly fold into berry mixture. Pour into the crumb-lined pan. Sprinkle with reserved crumbs.
- Cover and freeze until very firm, at least 12 hours.
- Garnish with berries and cut into wedges. Return any unused portion to freezer.
Serves 10-12.

Unbelievably Smooth and Creamy Cheesecake

1½ pounds cream cheese
1½ cups sugar
1 teaspoon vanilla
½ teaspoon fresh lemon juice

4 eggs
1 pint sour cream
3 tablespoons sugar
1 teaspoon vanilla

Crust:
2 cups graham crackers
¼ pound butter

¼ cup sugar

For best results, this cheesecake should be made 2 days in advance.

- Blend cream cheese and 1½ cups sugar until smooth. Add eggs one at a time.
- Add 1 teaspoon vanilla and lemon juice. Beat for 10 minutes.
- Add sour cream, 3 tablespoons sugar, and rest of vanilla. Beat 10 minutes more.

Crust:
- Crush crackers until ground.
- Cream butter and sugar with hands. Add crackers. Blend well.
- In a 9 or 10" springform pan spread the mixture on the bottom and half way up the sides with a spoon.
- Pour in mixture. Bake in 350° oven for 45 to 55 minutes. Turn off oven and leave cake in oven for 30 minutes with the door open. **Serves 12.**

Chocolate Cheesecake

Best served the day it is made.

1 package (9 ounces) chocolate wafers, crushed
½ stick butter
12 ounces semi-sweet chocolate
½ cup strong hot coffee

2 packages (8 ounces) cream cheese, softened
4 eggs
1 cup sugar
2 teaspoons vanilla
whipping cream

- Melt butter and stir in crushed wafers. Pat into 8" springform pan on the sides and bottom.
- Melt chocolate with coffee and mix well.
- Beat cream cheese, eggs, sugar, and vanilla together.
- Stir in chocolate mixture, and pour into pan.
- Bake at 325° for 55 minutes. Turn off oven, but don't remove cheesecake for 2-3 hours. DON'T PEEK!
- Serve with whipped cream.
  Serves 12.

Chocolate Peanut Butter Cheesecake

Crust:

1½ cups crushed chocolate
  wafers
1 tablespoon sugar

2 tablespoons unsalted butter,
  melted

Filling:

1 pound cream cheese, room
  temperature
1½ cups sugar
⅔ cup creamy peanut butter
5 eggs

½ cup sour cream
2 teaspoons fresh lemon juice
1 cup semi-sweet chocolate
  chips

Topping:

1 cup sour cream
¾ cup semi-sweet chocolate
  chips, melted

½ cup sugar

*This cheesecake
freezes beautifully.*

Crust:
- Combine all ingredients. Press firmly onto bottom and sides of greased 9" springform pan.
- Refrigerate 30 minutes.

Filling:
- Combine all ingredients except chips in food processor and blend until smooth.
- Mix in chips by hand. Pour into firm crust. Bake 70-80 minutes at 350°, until center is firm.
- Remove and let stand 15 minutes before adding topping.

Topping:
- Blend all ingredients thoroughly. Spread over warm cheesecake. Bake 10 minutes in 350° oven.
- Remove. Let cool for 1 hour at room temperature. Refrigerate at least 3 hours before removing from pan.
  Serves 12.

Bread Pudding with Drunken Sauce

6 jumbo croissants
3 cups milk
1 cup heavy cream
3 eggs
1½ cups lightly packed brown
  sugar
¼ teaspoon nutmeg

½ teaspoon cinnamon
2 tablespoons vanilla
1½ cups raisins
2 medium apples, peeled and
  chopped
2 tablespoons butter

Sauce:
1 egg
1 stick of butter
1 cup powdered sugar

¼ cup Rum, Bourbon or
  Amaretto

- Tear croissants into medium size pieces. Place in large bowl. Cover with milk and cream. Let stand ½ hour.
- Beat together eggs, sugar, vanilla, and spices. Add to moistened bread.
- Mix in raisins and apples.
- Pour into a greased 9x13 pan. Bake at 325° for 1 hour and 10 minutes.

Sauce:
- Melt butter, sugar, and egg in a double boiler. Whisk thoroughly.
- Take off heat. Add liquor. Pour over hot bread pudding. Serve warm.
  Serves 12.

A special thank you to
Linda Bosse of Slight Indulgence
for another wonderful recipe.

Peach Cobbler

3 pounds frozen sliced peaches
2 cups sugar
⅛ teaspoon clove
⅛ teaspoon nutmeg
⅛ teaspoon allspice

1 teaspoon vanilla
1½ teaspoons cinnamon
⅔ recipe of shortbread,
*   uncooked and softened*

Shortbread:
1 egg
1⅓ cups sugar
1 tablespoon vanilla

¾ pound butter, softened
3¼ cups flour
1 cup sliced raw almonds

- Put all ingredients except for the shortbread in a large skillet. Simmer for 20 minutes over medium heat.
- Pour mixture into a 9x13 greased pan. Crumble ⅔ of shortbread mixture evenly over the top.
- Bake at 350° for 45 minutes or until golden brown.
- Serve warm with heavy cream or half and half.

Shortbread:
- Cream egg, sugar, vanilla, and butter together. Slowly add the flour until well blended. Add almonds for the last minute of mixing. **Serves 12.**

Another terrific recipe from
Linda Bosse of Slight Indulgence.

Pumpkin Roll

3 eggs
1 cup white sugar
⅔ cup canned pumpkin
1 teaspoon baking soda

2 teaspoons pumpkin pie spice
1 teaspoon lemon juice
¾ cup flour
1 cup pecans, finely chopped

Filling:

1 package (8 ounces) cream
  cheese, softened
1 cup powdered sugar

1 teaspoon vanilla
4 tablespoons butter or
  margarine

- Cream eggs until light and fluffy. Gradually fold in the sugar, pumpkin and lemon juice.
- Fold in flour, baking soda and pumpkin pie spice.
- Pour into well greased jelly roll pan (15x10x2). Sprinkle with 1 cup nuts.
- Bake at 375° for 15 minutes. Quickly loosen sides with knife and turn the cake onto a thin towel sprinkled generously with powdered sugar.
- Roll the cake and towel together, rolling from the wide side.
- Let cool completely, then unroll and spread with cream cheese filling. Reroll.

Filling:
- Mix all ingredients together and use as directed above.
- Can be refrigerated or frozen. Slice when ready to serve.
  Serves 12.

Marzipan Cake with Raspberry Sauce

¼ pound butter or margarine
⅔ cup sugar
1 can (8 ounces) almond paste
4 large eggs
3 tablespoons flour

¼ teaspoon salt
¼ teaspoon baking powder
2 tablespoons kirsch or orange juice

Sauce:
½ cup seedless raspberry jam
¼ cup sugar
½ cup water

1 teaspoon kirsch
⅔ cup fresh raspberries

- Grease 9" cake pan, line with wax paper and grease again.
- Cream sugar and butter till fluffy.
- Add crumbled almond paste and beat at low speed 2-3 minutes.
- Separate eggs and add yolks one at a time to batter. Add kirsch or orange juice and continue beating.
- Beat in flour, salt, and baking powder.
- Whip egg whites till stiff and fold into batter.
- Pour into prepared cake pan and bake 300° for 45-60 minutes or until top springs back to a light touch.
- Carefully turn out and remove paper while cake is still warm. Eat plain or top with fresh raspberry sauce. Slice thin as the cake is rich.

Sauce:
- Combine jam, sugar and water in small sauce pan and boil for 3 minutes.
- Remove from heat and add kirsch or ¼ teaspoon almond extract.
- Cool and fold in fresh raspberries.
- Serve chilled.
  Serves 12-14.

Macaroon Ice Cream Cake

Try using different flavors of ice cream, such as coffee.

3 cups macaroon crumbs
1 quart vanilla ice cream, softened
½ cup melted butter
1 quart chocolate ice cream, softened

½ cup chopped nuts
½ pint whipping cream, whipped
1 cup finely chopped semi-sweet chocolate chips
slivered toasted almonds

- Combine crumbs, butter, chocolate and nuts.
- Using ¼ crumb mixture, make an even layer on bottom of 8" springform pan. Spread with ½ the vanilla ice cream. Add another layer of crumbs and freeze.
- When firm, spread with ½ the chocolate ice cream and another layer of crumbs. Freeze.
- Repeat for two more layers.
- Frost with whipped cream and almonds. Keep in freezer until serving time.
  Serves 8-12.

Chocolate Surprise Cake

A favorite with kids!

1½ cups sugar
3 eggs
1 cup salad oil
2 cans (10.5 ounces) beets, drained and pureed in blender

2 squares (4 ounces) semi-sweet baking chocolate or chips, melted
1¾ cups flour
1½ teaspoons soda
½ teaspoon salt
1 teaspoon vanilla

- Using an electric mixer, cream sugar and eggs.
- Add oil and beets.
- Add the melted baking chocolate.
- Sift together flour, soda and salt. Add to liquid mixture. Add vanilla.
- Grease and flour a 9x13 pan. Bake at 350° for 35-45 minutes.
- Cool and frost.
  Serves 12.

Chocolate Citrus Cake

1 cup sugar
1/2 cup butter
1/4 cup orange liqueur
1/4 cup water
1 package (18.25 ounces)
   Devil's food cake mix
1 cup sour cream
1 package (4 ounces) instant
   chocolate fudge pudding mix
4 eggs

1/2 cup vegetable oil
1/2 cup water
1/4 cup coffee liqueur
2 tablespoons fresh orange
   peel, grated
1 teaspoon ground cinnamon
1 package (12 ounces)
   chocolate chips
powdered sugar

- Combine first four ingredients in heavy, small saucepan. Stir over low heat until butter melts and sugar dissolves, about 3 minutes.
- Increase heat. Boil for 2 minutes. Cool completely.
- Preheat oven to 350°. Grease and cocoa a 10 cup bundt pan.
- Beat cake mix and next 8 ingredients until well blended, about 3 minutes.
- Stir in chocolate chips. Pour batter into prepared pan.
- Bake approximately 1 hour. Check with inserted toothpick. It should have a few moist crumbs attached when checked in the middle.
- Immediately spoon sugar and butter mixture over cake in pan. Let cake stand 30 minutes.
- Turn cake out onto platter. Cool completely. Sprinkle top with powdered sugar and serve.
Serves 10.

Fudge Delight

To serve this
luscious dessert,
spoon warm onto
plates, top with
ice cream or
whipped cream,
and hot fudge
sauce. Garnish
with nuts if
desired.

1½ cups (9 ounces) chocolate
  chips
⅔ cup butter or margarine
4 large eggs, separated at
  room temperature

⅓ cup flour
⅓ cup sugar
½ cup walnut or pecans
1 teaspoon vanilla
¼ teaspoon salt

Hot Fudge Sauce:

½ cup sugar
½ cup cocoa
½ cup cream
½ cup (3 ounces) chocolate
  chips

¼ cup butter or margarine,
  softened
1 teaspoon vanilla

- Preheat oven to 350°.
- Butter a 9" pie tin.
- In a heavy kettle, melt butter and chocolate over low heat, stirring constantly until smooth. Remove from heat.
- Stir yolks in one at a time until well mixed.
- Stir in flour, salt and vanilla.
- With an electric mixer at high speed, beat egg whites until foamy.
- Gradually beat in sugar until stiff peaks form.
- Fold chocolate mixture into beaten whites only until no streaks of white remain.
- Quickly fold in nuts and pour into greased pan.
- Bake 25 minutes. The center of the cake will be soft, will fall slightly, and crack on top.

Hot Fudge Sauce:

- In a heavy saucepan combine sugar and cocoa. Stir in cream until well mixed.
- Add chips and butter. Cook over LOW heat stirring constantly until sugar dissolves and sauce is smooth.
- Remove from heat and stir in vanilla. Pour into small pitcher to serve immediately. If made ahead, cover and refrigerate. Reheat over low heat before serving.
  Serves 6-8.

Strawberry Delight

4 eggs
½ cup flour
1 teaspoon baking powder
4 tablespoons milk
½ cup shortening
1¼ cups sugar
1 teaspoon vanilla

¾ cup walnuts, finely chopped
1 cup whipping cream, whipped
1½ cups sliced strawberries,
* well drained*
2 tablespoons powdered sugar
toasted sliced almonds

Try this with kiwis, peaches, or other fruits when strawberries are not in season.

- Grease 2 (8") round pans. Dust with flour. Preheat oven to 350°.
- Combine 4 egg yolks, flour, baking powder, milk, shortening and ½ cup sugar in a bowl. Beat with mixer until smooth. Spread in prepared pans.
- Beat 4 egg whites until stiff. Gradually add ¾ cup sugar. Fold in vanilla and walnuts. Spread this mixture over the thin cake batter in both pans.
- Bake at 350° for ½ hour. Cool.
- Place one layer on plate, egg whites down. Top with mixture of 1 cup whipping cream, powdered sugar, and sliced strawberries.
- Top with other layer and garnish with whipping cream, few sliced strawberries and sliced toasted almonds.
  Serves 10-12.

Frozen Mocha Pie

Crust:

1 cup flour

½ cup butter, softened

2 tablespoons sugar

¼ teaspoon salt

Filling:

6 ounces semi-sweet chocolate

1 package (8 ounces) cream
  cheese

⅓ cup packed brown sugar

1 tablespoon powdered instant
  coffee crushed

⅛ teaspoon salt

1 teaspoon vanilla

2 eggs, separated

¼ cup packed brown sugar

2 cups heavy cream, whipped

1 milk chocolate bar

Crust:
- Mix ingredients until crumbly.
- Press into 9" pie plate and bake in 375° for 12-15 minutes. Cool.

Filling:
- Melt semi-sweet chocolate.
- Beat cheese, ⅓ cup brown sugar, coffee, salt and vanilla until smooth.
- Add melted chocolate and egg yolks.
- Beat egg whites on high speed until soft peaks form. Beat in ¼ cup brown sugar until stiff peaks form.
- Fold egg whites into chocolate mixture.
- Reserve ½ cup whipped cream and fold remaining whipped cream into chocolate mixture.
- Pour into pie shell and freeze for at least 4 hours.
- Remove from freezer ½ an hour before serving.
- Sweeten reserved whipped cream with a teaspoon of brown sugar. Mound on pie.
- Garnish with milk chocolate bar curls. Use a potato peeler to make curls.
  Serves 8-10.

Irish Cream Pie

1½ cups chocolate wafer
  cookie crumbs (24 wafers)
¼ cup sugar
3 tablespoons butter, melted
½ cup Bailey's Irish Cream
  liqueur

2 tablespoons dark crème de
  cacao
1 quart vanilla ice cream,
  softened

Decadent!

Hot fudge sauce:
2 cups powdered sugar
1 cup + 2 tablespoons light
  corn syrup

2 sticks unsalted butter
6½ ounces unsweetened
  chocolate

- Combine cookie crumbs and sugar in medium bowl. Using a fork, stir in melted butter.
- Press mixture into bottom and sides of 9" pie plate.
- Mix liqueurs into softened ice cream and spoon into prepared crust.
- Freeze for at least 2 hours or 2 days ahead. Cover tightly with foil.

Hot fudge sauce:
- Cook all ingredients in double boiler until smooth, stirring often.
- Cover and refrigerate. Rewarm over simmering water. This can be made up to 3 days ahead.
- Serve sauce warm over pie.
  Serves 10-12.

Pumpkin Cranberry Pie

½ cup cranberry sauce, whole
1 pastry shell, 9"
1½ cups pumpkin
½ cup brown sugar

3 eggs
1¼ cups evaporated milk
2 teaspoons pumpkin pie spice
¼ teaspoon salt

- Place cranberry sauce in bottom of pie shell. Set aside.
- Mix other ingredients. Beat until smooth.
- Pour over cranberry sauce.
- Bake at 400° for 50 minutes or until knife comes out clean. Cool.
  Serves 8.

Cranberry Pie

Filling:
2 cups fresh cranberries   ½ cup chopped walnuts
½ cup sugar

Topping:
2 eggs   1 cup flour
1 cup sugar   1½ sticks butter, melted

Filling:
- Grease 10" pie pan. Spread cranberries over bottom. Sprinkle with nuts and sugar.

Topping:
- Beat eggs well. Add 1 cup sugar gradually. Beat until thoroughly mixed.
- Add flour and melted butter. Mix well.
- Pour over top of cranberries. (It is thick.)
- Bake at 325° for 1 hour or until golden brown.
- Serve warm with ice cream.
Serves 8.

Arboretum Lemon Forsythia Pie

Crust:
1 cup flour   2 tablespoons sugar
½ cup butter   ¼ teaspoon salt

Filling:
2 egg whites   ¼ cup lemon juice
⅔ cup sugar   1 cup heavy cream
2 teaspoons grated lemon peel   5 drops yellow food coloring

Crust:
- Mix flour, butter, sugar and salt until crumbly.
- Place ⅓ cup in a baking dish. Press the remainder into a 9" greased and floured pie tin.
- Bake both crumbs and crust at 375° for 12-15 minutes. Cool.

Filling:
- Combine egg whites, sugar, lemon peel, lemon juice, and food coloring in a mixing bowl. Beat until stiff, about 15 minutes.
- Whip cream. Fold into lemon mixture.
- Pour into cooled shell. Top with baked crumbs. Chill or freeze.
Serves 6-8.

Peanut Butter Pie

½ cup chunky peanut butter
4 ounces cream cheese,
* softened*
¼ cup powdered sugar

1 tub (8 ounces) of Cool Whip,
* thawed*
chocolate shavings
1 chocolate crust

- Mix all ingredients together by hand. Pour into crust.
- Freeze and remove 30 minutes before serving.
- Garnish with chocolate shavings.
  Serves 8.

Frosty Crème De Menthe

1 quart rich vanilla ice cream
½ cup green Crème De Menthe

¼ cup Irish liqueur

- Blend all ingredients until smooth.
- Fill pretty glass cups and freeze ahead.
- Garnish with whipping cream, mint leaves, fresh fruit, or chocolate shavings.
  Serves 10.

Quick and easy to do ahead for company.

Crème De Menthe Bars

Crust:

½ cup margarine
4 tablespoons cocoa
½ cup powdered sugar
1 egg
1 teaspoon vanilla

2 cups crushed graham
  crackers
1½ cups chopped nuts
1 cup coconut

Filling:

½ cup margarine
3 tablespoons Crème De
  Menthe

2 teaspoons instant vanilla
  pudding
2 cups powdered sugar

Frosting:

½ cup margarine

2 cups chocolate chips

Crust:
- Melt margarine and cocoa together over low heat. Cool. Add powdered sugar.
- Beat egg with vanilla. Add to above.
- Mix crackers, nuts, and coconut together. Add to above.
- Press into 9x13 lightly greased pan. Refrigerate 1-2 hours.

Filling:
- Add remaining ingredients to melted butter. Beat until smooth. Spread on crust.

Frosting:
- Melt margarine and chips over low heat. Spread over top. Refrigerate until top is hard. Check after 45 minutes.
- Cut into small bars.
  Makes 75 bars.

Grand Chocolate Mint Squares

Stage I:

1 cup sugar	*4 eggs*
1 cup butter or margarine,	*½ teaspoon salt*
softened	*1 teaspoon vanilla*
1 cup flour	*1 can Hershey syrup (16 ounces)*

Stage II:

2 cups powdered sugar	*½ cup butter or margarine,*
2 tablespoons crème de menthe	*softened*

Stage III:

6 ounces chocolate chips	*6 tablespoons butter*

Stage I:
- Mix all ingredients together. Bake in greased 9x13 pan for 30 minutes at 350°. Cool completely.

Stage II:
- Mix all ingredients together. Spread over cool brownies. Put in freezer to harden for 10 minutes.

Stage III:
- Melt ingredients together. Cool and spread over brownies.
  Makes 24.

Lemon Blueberry Mousse

4 egg yolks	*2 egg whites, stiffly beaten*
½ cup sugar	*½ cup whipped heavy cream*
5 tablespoons lemon juice	*½ cup fresh blueberries*
2 teaspoons grated lemon rind	

- Beat the four egg yolks until thick and pale.
- Beat in sugar, lemon juice and rind. Cook mixture in double boiler, stirring constantly, until thick. Cool.
- Fold in the two stiffly beaten egg whites, the whipped heavy cream, and the blueberries.
- Pour into stemmed glasses or brandy snifters. Garnish with mint leaves and more blueberries. Chill thoroughly.
  Serves 4.

Chocolate Raspberry Trifle

Decorate with orange slices, strips of orange peel, fresh pitted cherries, or chocolate curls, if desired.

1 pound cake, 16 ounces
1 jar (16 ounces) raspberry jam
¼ cup Kirschwasser
5 tablespoons Grand Marnier
3¾ cups whipping cream
1 vanilla pudding mix (5.1 ounces)
6 ounces semi-sweet chocolate

4 ounces sweet chocolate
1 teaspoon vanilla
3 tablespoons sugar
4 eggs, separated
2 egg yolks
⅛ teaspoon salt
2 tablespoons fresh orange juice

- Prepare the vanilla pudding according to the package directions. Chill.
- In a food processor, chop 4 ounces each of semi-sweet and sweet chocolate together. Add 2 tablespoons of Grand Marnier, 1 teaspoon vanilla, and ⅛ teaspoon of salt. Process until smooth.
- Scald 1 cup whipping cream over low heat. Add to chocolate mixture. Process until chocolate is melted.
- Add 4 egg yolks and process again. Pour into large mixing bowl. Chill 15 minutes.
- Beat 4 egg whites until they hold firm peaks. Fold into chocolate mixture gently by hand. Return to refrigerator. This is the chocolate mousse.
- Combine 2 egg yolks, 3 tablespoons sugar, 3 tablespoons Grand Marnier, and 2 tablespoons orange juice in the top of a double boiler. Whisk over boiling water until thick.
- Melt 2 ounces semi-sweet chocolate in small saucepan over low heat. Stir it into the egg yolk mixture. Pour into a large mixing bowl. Chill 20 minutes.
- Whip ¾ cup whipping cream until it holds firm peaks. Fold into the chocolate mixture gently by hand. Return to refrigerator. This is the chocolate cream.
- Slice the pound cake into ¼" slices. Line bottom and sides of a 12" diameter (or larger) glass bowl with half the slices.
- Sprinkle slices with ⅛ cup Kirschwasser. Spread half the raspberry jam on top. Pour in the vanilla pudding.
- Place ¼ of slices over pudding. Sprinkle with half the remaining Kirschwasser. Spread on half the remaining jam. Pour in the chocolate mousse.
- Place the remaining slices on top. Sprinkle with remaining Kirschwasser. Spread on remaining jam. Pour in chocolate cream.
- Chill overnight.
- Whip 2 cups of whipping cream until it forms firm peaks. Spread over entire trifle.
Serves 12.

Lemon Sours

First layer:

½ cup sugar

¾ cup butter, softened

1½ cups flour

Second layer:

2 eggs

¼ teaspoon salt

¼ teaspoon baking powder

1 cup brown sugar

1 cup pecans, chopped

2 tablespoons crushed
   pineapple

2 tablespoons cranberry relish

Third layer:

juice of 1 large lemon

1 lemon peel, finely grated

1 tablespoon butter, softened

1¼ cups powdered sugar

- Grease and flour 9x13x3 inch pan.
- First layer: Mix all ingredients together and press into bottom of pan. Bake 15 minutes at 350°.
- Second layer: Process all ingredients in blender until nuts are chopped finely, but not pureed. Spoon over first layer and bake 20 minutes at 325°. Let cool slightly.
- Third layer: Beat ingredients together with mixer until of spreading consistency. Spread over warm cookies. Let cool and cut into squares.
  Makes 20 bars.

These freeze well, and are a favorite with everyone.

Carrot Cookies

1 cup sugar

1 egg

¾ cup shortening

1 teaspoon vanilla

1 cup carrots, cooked and
   mashed

2 cups flour

½ teaspoon salt

2 teaspoons baking powder

1½ cups powdered sugar

1 orange

Nutritious and delicious!

- Mix all ingredients except powdered sugar and orange together.
- Roll dough into tablespoon size balls and place on ungreased cookie sheet.
- Bake 10-12 minutes at 400°. Cool.
- Mix powdered sugar, rind of orange, and juice needed to make smooth frosting.
- Frost cookies after they are cooled.
  Makes 2 dozen.

Date Bars

1 cup sugar
3 eggs, 2 whole and 1 egg
  white
2 cups dates, chopped
1 cup nut meats, broken
1 cup flour

1 teaspoon baking powder
⅛ teaspoon salt
¼ teaspoon cloves
¼ teaspoon cinnamon
1 teaspoon vanilla
powdered sugar

- Beat eggs until light. Gradually add in sugar.
- Add dates and nuts.
- Sift the flour, baking powder, salt, cloves, and cinnamon together.
- Add the sifted ingredients to the egg mixture along with the vanilla.
- Beat the batter until the ingredients are well blended. Pour into a greased and floured 9x13 pan.
- Bake at 325° for about 25 minutes. Cut when cooled and roll in powdered sugar.
- These stay fresh for several days when wrapped in saran wrap. They also freeze easily.
  Makes 24 bars.

Mixed Nut Bars

These bars taste like candy, and are fun at a casual outing.

Try substituting a can of Honey Roast Nut mix.

1½ cups flour
¾ cup sugar
½ cup butter
½ teaspoon salt
2 tablespoons butter

½ cup white Karo syrup
1 tablespoon water
1 package (12 ounces)
  butterscotch chips
1 can (12 ounces) mixed nuts

- Cut flour into sugar, ½ cup butter, and salt till crumbly.
- Press mixture into 9x13 pan and bake for 12 minutes at 350°. Cool.
- Melt 2 tablespoons butter, syrup, water, and chips over low heat.
- Spread on the cooled, baked crust.
- Sprinkle with nuts on top, pressing them lightly into the mixture.
- Refrigerate and cool.
  Serves 16-20.

Praline Topping

2 tablespoons soft butter
¼ cup firmly packed brown
   sugar

½ cup coarsely chopped pecans

*Terrific with
pumpkin pie.*

- Mix butter and brown sugar in small skillet over medium heat until bubbly.
- Add pecans. Cook, stirring constantly, for 2 minutes.
- Remove from heat. Turn out onto lightly greased foil. Cool.
- Crumble into small pieces. Refrigerate.
- Serve as a garnish over pies with whipped cream.
  Serves 8.

Brandied Apples

4 cups semi-sweet apples,
   sliced and peeled
¼ cup butter

½-¾ cup brown sugar,
   depending on tartness of
   apples
2-3 tablespoons brandy

*Delicious too as a
side dish for
brunch or with
pork.*

- Mix all ingredients in 6x9 pan. Bake in a 350° oven for 15-30 minutes or until tender.
- Cover with foil if rewarming.
- Wonderful served over French vanilla ice cream.
  Serves 4-6.

Fiesta Favorites

*Ten years ago, The Junior League of Phoenix set about publishing another cookbook, **Fiesta Under the Sun**. The enormous success of that first publishing endeavor and the wonderful recipes contained therein served to inspire us as we compiled **Desert Treasures**. Taste some of the favorites of Fiesta. They are as tantalizing now as they were when first presented.*

Fiesta Dip

1 can (16 ounces) refried beans
1 can (4 ounces) green chilies, chopped
1 carton (16 ounces) sour cream
1 tomato, chopped

2 cans frozen avocado dip (10 ounces each)
½ cup red onion, chopped
1 can (4 ounces) ripe olives, chopped
1 cup Cheddar cheese, grated
large round tostado or tortilla chips

- Layer the ingredients in the order listed on a 12" plate. Place the 12" plate on a large platter. Surround with chips.
  Serves 6-8.

Taco Soup

2-3 pounds lean beef
1 teaspoon salt
3-4 cans (7.5 ounces) taco sauce
1 can (7 ounces) green chile salsa

1 can (4 ounces) green chilies, diced
1 can (15 ounces) tomato sauce
garlic salt to taste

Garnishes:
chopped onions
chopped lettuce

grated Cheddar cheese
corn chips

- Brown beef with salt. Drain. Add all other ingredients. Bring to a boil. Simmer 30 minutes. It should be the consistency of chili.
- Spoon into bowls. Pass chips and other garnishes.
  Serves 8.

Hot Crab Dip

½ cup Monterey Jack cheese,
grated
¾ cup mayonnaise (don't use
salad dressing)
6 ounces crab meat

10 scallions, finely chopped
Worcestershire sauce
Tabasco sauce, 4-6 drops
salt to taste

- Combine all ingredients. Warm in chafing dish. Serve with crackers.
  Serves 6.

Nachos Grandes

½ pound ground beef
½ pound Chorizo sausage
1 large onion, chopped
salt
Tabasco sauce to taste
2 cans (16 ounces) refried
beans
1 can (4 ounces) green chilies,
chopped
1½ cups Monterey Jack cheese,
grated

1½ cups Cheddar cheese,
grated
¾ cup taco sauce
¼ cup green onion, chopped
1 ripe avocado, peeled and
mashed
1 cup sour cream
1 can (4.5 ounces) sliced ripe
olives

Serve with tortilla
chips around
edges of bean
mixture making a
petaled flower
effect. Keep warm
on a warming
tray.

Try using ground
turkey for a health
conscious choice.

- Remove casing from chorizo. Crumble with ground beef into heavy frying pan. Brown with onion. Drain and season with salt and Tabasco sauce.
- Spread beans in 10x15 baking dish. Top with meat mixture. Sprinkle with green chilies. Cover with cheeses. Drizzle taco sauce over top. This may be covered and refrigerated or frozen at this stage.
- Bake uncovered at 400° for 20-25 minutes or until heated through.
- Garnish with green onions and olives Mound avocado in the center and top with dollops of sour cream.
  Serves 12.

Chicken Chutney Salad

4 chicken breasts, cooked,
  boned, skinned, cut into bite
  size pieces
1 cup sliced celery

1 bunch green onions, chopped
1 can (11 ounces) pineapple
  tidbits, saving liquid
1 cup cashews

Dressing:
Juice from pineapple tidbits
½ cup sour cream
½ cup mayonnaise
1 teaspoon curry

2 teaspoons lime juice
¼ of 12.5 ounces jar of Major
  Grey Chutney, cut up

- Combine salad ingredients in a large bowl.
- Mix dressing ingredients together. Pour over salad. Mix well.
  Serves 8.

Kiwi-Avocado Salad

2 large, ripe avocados, peeled
  and quartered lengthwise
1 large orange, peeled and
  sectioned (save juice)
¼ cup lime juice
¼ teaspoon salt

2 tablespoons walnut oil
1 teaspoon honey
2 tablespoons light vegetable
  oil
4 kiwi fruits, peeled and thinly
  sliced crosswise

- Place one cut side of avocado on a board. Thinly slice across on the
  bias. Keeping slices together, slip onto serving platter. Fan out
  slices into graceful design. Repeat for each plate.
- Arrange orange slices decoratively around avocado.
- Combine lime juice, salt, walnut oil, honey, juice from orange and
  vegetable oil.
- Pour evenly over platters to cover thoroughly. Arrange kiwi slices
  over top. Chill, covered, up to 1 hour.
  Serves 8.

Sedona Salad

4 chicken breasts, boneless,
  skinless (cooked in strips)
½ pound Monterey Jack
  cheese, cut into strips
½ pound salami, cut into strips

12 slices of orange, peeled
12 slices of avocado
pitted ripe black olives
lettuce leaves

Cumin Dressing:
½ cup mayonnaise
½ cup sour cream
2 tablespoons lemon juice
⅛ teaspoon dry mustard

¼ teaspoon garlic salt
½ teaspoon cumin
4 tablespoons green chile salsa

- For individual servings, arrange lettuce leaves on plate. Arrange remaining salad ingredients. Cover and chill. At serving time add dressing.
- Blend together dressing ingredients until the flavors are mixed. **Serves 4.**

Marinated Broccoli

3 bunches broccoli, using
  flowerettes only
1 cup cider vinegar
1 tablespoon sugar
1 tablespoon dill weed

1 tablespoon Accent
1 teaspoon salt
1 teaspoon garlic salt
1 teaspoon pepper
1½ cups vegetable oil

Cool summer hors d'oeuvre with a different taste.

- Clean and drain broccoli pieces. Place in large bowl.
- Mix marinade ingredients together. Pour over broccoli.
- Refrigerate for at least 24 hours before serving. **Serves 6-8.**

Committee's Chalupas

3 pounds pork loin or butt,
  boneless and trimmed
2 garlic cloves, minced
1 teaspoon oregano
1 tablespoon plus 1 teaspoon
  ground cumin
1 teaspoon salt
1 can (16 ounces) tomatoes

2 cans (14.5 ounces) chicken
  broth
1 onion, chopped
2 cans (7 ounces) diced green
  chilies
1 pound pinto beans, rinsed
¼ teaspoon crushed red pepper
1 cup water or more if needed

Garnishes:

grated cheese
chopped onions
sour cream
guacamole or avocado slices
diced tomatoes

shredded lettuce
salsa
black olives
tortilla chips

- Place all ingredients in a 6-8 quart kettle. Bring to a boil. Reduce heat and simmer covered 3-6 hours. Stir often adding water as needed.
- Shred cooked pork. Serve over tortilla chips with garnishes. **Serves 12-16.**

Shrimp and Crabmeat Au Gratin

1 pound shrimp
2 tablespoons butter
2 tablespoons flour
1¼ cups milk
¼ teaspoon salt
1 pound lump crabmeat
1 teaspoon Dijon mustard
1 teaspoon Worcestershire
* sauce*

1 teaspoon hot sauce
1 cup mild Cheddar cheese,
* grated*
⅓ cup Monterey Jack cheese,
* grated*
2 tablespoons dry sherry
3 green onions, chopped
salt and pepper to taste
½ cup parsley, chopped

- Boil shrimp in salted water for 10 minutes or until done. Clean shrimp after cooking.
- Melt butter over low heat. Add flour. Stir until smooth. Add milk and salt. Stir constantly to avoid lumps. Cook until creamy.
- Add white sauce to mixture of all ingredients except crab, shrimp and parsley. Mix well.
- Fold in shrimp and crab.
- Pour into a buttered baking dish. Bake, uncovered, for 25 minutes at 350°.
- Sprinkle with parsley before serving. Serve over brown rice.
  Serves 6.

Spanish Rice

1 can (16 ounces) solid pack
  tomatoes
¾-1 cup white rice
1 cup Longhorn Cheddar
  cheese, chopped
1 jar (4 ounces) Spanish olives,
  chopped

¼ cup olive oil
½ cup onions, chopped
1¼ cups boiling water
1 teaspoon salt
2 ounces green chilies, chopped

- Mix all ingredients together. Place in a 2 quart casserole.
- Cover. Bake for 1 hour at 350°, stirring frequently.
  Serves 6-8.

Sedona Sesame Teriyaki Marinade

6 tablespoons sesame seeds
4 tablespoons sugar
2 tablespoons oil

6 tablespoons soy sauce
2 green onions, finely chopped
1 tablespoon flour

- Toast sesame seeds on cookie sheet at 325°. Turn frequently and watch carefully.
- Pulverize seeds in food processor or blender.
- Add remaining ingredients and mix.
- Marinate steak 15 minutes to overnight.

Satin Caramel Flan

*1 can Eagle Brand condensed
  milk (14 ounces)*
1½ cans fresh milk
4 eggs

1 teaspoon vanilla
¼ cup sugar
1 cup sugar for caramelizing

*Perfect ending to
a spicy meal.*

- Blend condensed milk, fresh milk, eggs, vanilla, and ¼ cup sugar together in a blender for 1 minute.
- Place 1 cup sugar in cast iron pan. Heat over medium heat until sugar is melted and brown. Pour into buttered 9x9 pan.
- Pour blended custard over caramel. Place in pan of water and bake 45-60 minutes in a 350° oven.
- Remove. Cool and chill.
- Invert onto a platter or spoon out individual servings. **Serves 6-8.**

Black Russian Cake

*1 yellow cake mix (18.25
  ounces)*
½ cup sugar
*1 box (6.5 ounces) chocolate
  instant pudding mix*
1 cup vegetable oil

4 eggs
¼ cup vodka
¼ cup Kahlúa
¾ cup water
Pam spray

Glaze:
½ cup powdered sugar

¼ cup Kahlúa

- Pour all liquid ingredients into dry ingredients at one time. Beat for 4 minutes.
- Pour mixture into sprayed bundt pan. Bake 45-50 minutes at 350°.
- Cool 10 minutes, then invert pan. Poke holes in the top so that glaze can soak into cake

Glaze:
- Mix together and let stand while cake is cooling. Pour over cake. Dust with extra powdered sugar. **Serves 8.**

Lemon Squares

¼ cup butter
½ cup Crisco
⅓ cup powdered sugar
1½ cups flour
3 eggs, slightly beaten

3 tablespoons flour
1½ cups sugar
¼-⅓ cup lemon juice
grated rind of lemon
powdered sugar

- Mix first 4 ingredients together. Bake in a 9x13 pan for 15-20 minutes at 350°. The edges should be pale tan.
- Mix remaining ingredients and pour on top of the crust. Bake 20 minutes or until custard is set. Sprinkle with powdered sugar. Cut into squares when cool.
Makes 4 dozen bars.

German Chocolate Caramel Bars

1 package (14 ounces)
  caramels
⅔ cup evaporated milk
1 German chocolate cake mix
  (18.25 ounces)

¾ cup butter or margarine,
  melted
1 cup walnuts, chopped
1 cup semi-sweet chocolate
  chips

- Heat caramels and ⅓ cup evaporated milk over low heat until caramels melt. Set aside.
- Stir together cake mix, butter, ⅓ cup evaporated milk, and walnuts. Batter will be thick.
- Spread ½ the batter in a greased 9x13 pan. Bake 6 minutes at 350°.
- Sprinkle chips over baked crust. Drizzle melted caramel mixture over chips. Spread remaining batter over top. It will not be smooth.
- Bake 15-18 minutes. Be careful not to overbake. Cool and refrigerate 30 minutes to set caramels. Serve at room temp.
Makes 4 dozen bars.

Chocolate Sherry Cream Bars

4 ounces baking chocolate
1 cup butter or margarine
4 eggs
2 cups sugar

½ teaspoon salt
1 teaspoon vanilla
1 cup sifted flour

Filling:
½ cup butter
4 cups powdered sugar
¼ cup cream

4 tablespoons sherry
1 cup nuts, chopped

Topping:
1 package (6 ounces)
   chocolate chips

3 tablespoons water
4 tablespoons butter

Beautiful at Christmas with red and green swirls on top.

- Preheat oven to 325°.
- Melt chocolate and butter in double boiler. Cool slightly.
- Beat eggs until light. Gradually add sugar. Then add the chocolate mixture, flour sifted with salt, and finally the vanilla. Beat 1 full minute.
- Pour into greased and lightly floured 10x14 pan. Bake 25 minutes and then cool.

Filling:
- Beat butter and sugar together.
- Gradually add cream and sherry.
- When light and fluffy, add nuts. Mix well.
- Spread over cooled base. Chill in refrigerator.

Topping:
- Melt chocolate chips with water and butter in a double boiler.
- Mix well, and dribble over filling. Let harden before cutting into bars.
  Makes 3-4 dozen.

Valley's Finest Chefs

Black and White Bean Soup

Health tip: When you overcook the beans, just a little, they are more easily digested.

1 cup small white beans
1 cup small black beans
½ cup each diced carrots, onions, celery, red pepper and green pepper
4 ounces Panchetta (Italian bacon) or regular smoked bacon, diced
4 smoked pork loin steaks

1 ham hock
2 quarts chicken stock
4 tablespoons olive oil
2 tablespoons vinegar
1 tablespoon fresh thyme
2 cloves garlic, finely diced
1 bunch parsley, chopped
1 bay leaf
salt and pepper to taste

- Soak beans overnight in warm water in two separate pots.
- Simmer beans separately (using half of the following ingredients) with ham hock, pork loins, bay leaf and thyme for 1½ hours or until soft. Set aside and remove meat.
- Sauté the panchetta in oil until golden brown. Add vegetables and cook until they are glazed.
- Add chicken stock. Cook on high for 5 minutes.
- Add vinegar and cooked beans. Simmer 15-25 minutes or until beans are soft and begin to fall apart.
- Remove meat from bones, cut into small cubes, and add to soup.
- Add parsley and season with pepper. Bring to boil and season with salt.
- Using two ladles, pour beans simultaneously side by side into the same bowl.
Serves 4.

A great recipe from Executive Chef Anton Brunbauer at the Hyatt Regency's Golden Swan in Scottsdale.

Pumpkin Soup

¼ cup butter
1 medium onion, diced
¼ cup flour
3 cloves garlic, chopped
3 shallots, chopped
½ bunch green onions, diced
½ teaspoon cumin
½ teaspoon oregano
½ teaspoon hot chili powder

½ teaspoon cayenne
1 tablespoon tomato paste
2 pounds pumpkin, banana or
   any hard yellow squash,
   peeled, seeded and chopped
4 cups chicken broth
½ bunch cilantro, finely
   chopped
¼ cup milk

Garnish with sour cream and fried tortilla strips.

- Sauté onions, green onions, and all spices except cilantro in butter, until onions are translucent.
- Using a wire whisk, add flour and cook without scorching for 12 minutes.
- Add hot chicken stock, squash, cilantro and tomato paste. Simmer until squash is soft.
- Pour into blender or food processor while still hot. Puree, then add milk and stir until hot.
  Serves 8.

A special thank you to Chef John Bartilomo of the 8700 Restaurant.

Cilantro Lime Vinaigrette

⅜ cup jalapeño peppers,
   chopped
¼ cup red bell pepper, diced
3 green onions, chopped
1 tablespoon cilantro, chopped

1 teaspoon garlic, chopped
3 ounces red wine vinegar
3 ounces fresh squeezed lime
   juice
2 cups salad oil

- Combine and blend thoroughly.
- Salt and pepper to taste.
- Use over greens or as a marinade for both vegetables and poultry.

This recipe is shared with us by the Registry Resort in Scottsdale.

Warm Grilled Seafood Salad with Cucumber Ginger Vinaigrette

*4 swordfish medallions (3
  ounces each)*
8 shrimp

8 sea scallops
assorted lettuce
4 plum tomatoes, sliced

Cucumber Ginger Vinaigrette:
*2 cucumbers, peeled, seeded
  and diced*
4 cloves garlic, chopped
4 shallots, chopped
4 teaspoons ginger, grated
4 Serrano chilies, chopped
1 bunch cilantro, chopped
2 red peppers, diced
2 yellow peppers, diced

2 cups rice vinegar
2 cups chicken stock
4 teaspoons sesame oil
4 teaspoons soy sauce
juice of 2 limes
3 teaspoons Dijon mustard
6 ounces olive oil
2 ounces honey

- Blend all liquid ingredients together.
- Mix in peppers, cilantro, chili, ginger, shallots, garlic and cucumber.
- Season to taste.
- Arrange assorted lettuce on the plate. Grill swordfish, shrimp and scallops.
- Place seafood over lettuce. Pour over the vinaigrette.
  Serves 4.

*** Thank you to the Ritz-Carlton in Phoenix
for sharing this recipe with us.***

Baby American Greens with Orange Honey Barbecued Salmon

6 salmon filets (3 ounces each)
1 cup orange honey barbecue
  sauce
baby American greens of
  choice (Frisse, Baby Red
  Oak, Mache Carrot Leaves)

¼ cup cider vinegar
¼ cup hazelnut oil
2 tablespoons fresh
  horseradish, grated

Serve with Desert Melon Soup.

If you can't find fresh horseradish, use bottled.

Orange Honey Barbecue Sauce:

1 cup ketchup
1 cup honey
¼ cup Dijon Mustard
¼ cup jalapeño peppers,
  chopped
2 tablespoons Japanese rice
  vinegar
1 tablespoon Tabasco
3 tablespoons brown sugar

1 tablespoon curry
½ tablespoon paprika
1 teaspoon soy sauce
1 teaspoon garlic, chopped
1 teaspoon vegetable oil
½ teaspoon Worchestershire
  sauce
½ teaspoon lemon juice
¼ teaspoon ground pepper

- Dip salmon in barbeque sauce. Sauté or grill for approximately three minutes per side.
- Place washed greens on plate. Add salmon. Sprinkle with oil and vinegar. Garnish with horseradish.

Sauce:
- Mix all ingredients and chill.
  Serves 6.

Special thanks to the Squash Blossom
at the Hyatt Regency Scottsdale
and Executive Chef Anton Brunbauer.

Vitello Gaetano

*3 veal scallopini (2 ounces
  each)*
3 eggplant slices, 3x½"
*3 Mozzarella cheese slices,
  1x2"*
3 proscuitto slices, 1x2"
3 ounces pasta

¼ cup dry Marsala wine
¼ cup butter
2 mushrooms, sliced
2 tablespoons white wine
2 tablespoons olive oil
2 tablespoons Marinara sauce
salt and pepper, dash

- Pound veal into thin slices. Dust lightly in flour and sear on both sides in hot oil.
- Place eggplant on top of veal followed by proscuitto and Mozzarella.
- Deglaze pan with white wine, Marsala, pepper and marinara sauce.
- Simmer for 30 seconds. Add butter and mushrooms. Simmer for 30 seconds. Place under broiler until cheese melts.
- Serve on plate with your favorite pasta and garnish.
  Serves 1.

Special thanks to Executive Chef Anton Brunbauer
of Ristorante Sandolo at the Hyatt Regency Scottsdale.

Southwestern Grilled Veal Medallions

12 medallions (2 ounces) veal loin

Relish:

2 cups black beans
3 ears of sweet corn
*½ cup chicken stock or one
  chicken bouillon cube*
*¼ fresh jalapeño or ¼ cup
  chopped pickled jalapeño*

1 small red onion, diced
4 medium tomatillos, diced
1 medium red pepper, diced
¼ cup cilantro, chopped

Vinaigrette:

*4 tablespoons prickly pear
  cactus jelly*
4 tablespoons jalapeño juice
4 tablespoons lemon juice
⅛ teaspoon shallots, minced

⅛ teaspoon garlic, minced
4 ounces red wine vinegar
4 ounces olive oil
pinch of white pepper

Garnish:

Four leaves baby lettuce
Four leaves red oak lovia rosa

Four leaves frises red romaine

Relish:
- Cook black beans until tender in chicken stock, water and chopped jalapeños. Completely cover beans with water while boiling. Rinse thoroughly until water is clear. Chill.
- Roast corn on outdoor grill or in oven on broil. Monitor closely and turn corn frequently until husk is well browned. Chill.
- Remove husk and kernels. Chill kernels.
- Place beans, corn and all other relish ingredients in a bowl. Mix well with half of the vinaigrette.

Vinaigrette:
- Place cactus jelly, shallots, garlic, jalapeño juice, lemon juice and rice wine vinegar in a medium mixing bowl. Mix well with whisk.
- Slowly add olive oil while whisking. Finish with a pinch of white pepper.
- Flavor with more jalapeño juice if desired.

Veal:
- Grill to 130°, making diamond shapes on both sides.

Presentation:
- Use one of each leaf of the four lettuce leaves. Place in the upper left hand corner of the plate at the 10 and 11 o'clock position. Place the relish in the center of the plate, with the medallions half on the relish. Place the medallions evenly spaced at the 2, 5, and 7 o'clock positions. Drizzle vinaigrette on top of veal and lettuce. Enjoy.

Serves 4.

***Thank you to Chef Larry Marcus of the Chaparral Room
at the Camelback Inn for sharing his recipe with us.***

Salmone Affrunicato

1 ounce smoked salmon
juice of ½ a lemon

2 tablespoons pesto
  mayonnaise
10 capers

Pesto Mayonnaise:
½ cup pesto sauce

1½ cup mayonnaise

- Blend ingredients together in blender or food processor until a creamy consistency.
- Accompany with Vitello Gaetano and an Italian salad.
  Serves 1.

Another fabulous recipe from
Executive Chef Anton Brunbauer of the
Ristorante Sandolo at the Hyatt Regency Scottsdale.

"Choucroute" with Champagne

1 medium onion
¼ cup duck fat
1 clove garlic, chopped
2 cups dry white wine
1 medium apple, sliced very
  thin
2 small bay leaves
12-18 juniper berries
1½ pounds sauerkraut, drained

2 red potatoes
2 slices cooked ham, thinly
  sliced
2 Strasbourg sausages (or a
  good quality wiener)
sliced pork loin, sautéed in
  duck fat, seasoned with salt,
  pepper, and garlic
3 slices garlic sausage

Chef Jean-Marie recommends serving with a fruity white wine preferably from Alsace Lorraine.

- Sauté onion in duck fat until golden. Add garlic. Stir for 1 minute.
- Add wine, apple, bay leaves, berries, and sauerkraut. Keep at a slow boil until reduced by two-thirds. Reserve.
- Prepare meats while steaming red potatoes.
- Place the "Choucroute" in the bottom of a shallow dish. Arrange the meats tastefully on top. Add steamed potatoes, cut into wedges. Sprinkle chopped parsley on potatoes. Serve with Dijon mustard. **Serves 2.**

Special thank you to
Chef Jean-Marie Rigollet of Marché Gourmet.

Bouillabaisse, J-MR's Style

1 medium onion
2 tablespoons olive oil
2 cloves garlic, chopped
2 medium red potatoes, sliced
1/16" thick
½ bunch fresh parsley,
coarsely chopped
2 medium tomatoes, cut in 6
wedges each
3 large sprigs of fresh thyme
2 pinches fennel seeds

salt and pepper to taste
.008 ounces saffron
1 quart fish stock or clam juice
⅓ cup tomato sauce
1 pound fish filets (red snapper
is best), cut into large cubes
1 cup scallops
1 cup bay shrimp
4 mussels
8 slice stale French bread

Rouille Sauce:
3 egg yolks
¾ cup olive oil
salt, pepper and garlic to taste

juice of ½ lemon
1 large tablespoons Harissa
pimiento paste

- Sauté onion in olive oil until light golden. Add garlic. Stir for 1 minute.
- Add potatoes. Reduce heat. Stir.
- Add parsley. Stir.
- Add tomatoes. Stir for 2 minutes.
- Add thyme, fennel seeds, salt, pepper, and saffron. Stir.
- Add fish stock and tomato sauce. Increase heat and bring to a low boil.
- When potatoes are done, add filet cubes. Simmer 5-8 minutes.
- Add scallops, bay shrimp, and mussels. Stir. Simmer 4 minutes.
- Taste and adjust seasonings. Reserve.

Rouille Sauce:
- Make fresh mayonnaise using yolks and olive oil.
- Add salt, pepper, garlic, lemon juice, and pimiento paste.

To Serve:
- Place 4 slices of stale bread into the bottom of soup plate. Ladle the "Bouillabaisse" over the bread. Distribute the "Rouille" sauce over to spice up your dish. Serve with a crisp white wine.

Another great recipe from
Chef Jean-Marie Rigollet of Marché Gourmets.

Grilled Quail Breast in Phyllo with Caper Herb Lemon Butter

8 quail breasts, skin on
2 leeks
1 large carrot
1 large zucchini
1 large yellow squash
1 bunch green onions

10 Shiitake mushroom caps
2 shallots
2 cups clarified butter
1 box phyllo dough
salt and pepper to taste

Sauce:

1 tablespoon shallot, chopped
2 cups white wine
1 tablespoon capers
½ pound whole unsalted
   butter, melted

1 tablespoon fresh parsley,
   chopped
1 tablespoon fresh basil,
   chopped

Can substitute chicken breasts or veal tenders for the quail.

- Julienne all vegetables. Set aside some julienned leeks to tie pouches. Sauté leeks, shallots, and shiitake mushrooms for 2 minutes. Add remaining vegetables.
- Season and cook for 2 minutes. Set aside at room temperature.
- Grill seasoned quail breasts until done, approximately 3-4 minutes. Set aside at room temperature.
- Butter phyllo dough sheets one at a time, layering them one on top of the other until there are 7 layers. Prepare a total of 4 stacks.
- Place one quail breast on one stack of phyllo. Place vegetable mixture on top of quail. Shape into a pouch, trimming edges if necessary. Tie with a blanched leek. Bake for 20 minutes in a 350° oven.

Sauce:

- Reduce wine with shallots until only 1 tablespoon remains. Add herbs and capers.
- Whisk in butter until thickened to a syrup consistency.
- To serve, place sauce in serving plate and place phyllo pouch onto sauce.
Serves 4.

*Another great recipe from
the Scottsdale Conference Center.*

Lobster Mousse and Spinach Roulade with Holland Pepper Chive Coulis

3 lobster tails, shelled
2 pounds fresh cleaned spinach
  leaves
1 pint heavy cream

2 tablespoons fresh basil,
  chopped
1 tablespoon fresh parsley,
  chopped
salt and white pepper to taste

Sauce:
2 large golden Holland
  peppers, seeded, and cut into
  1" pieces
6 cups light fish or chicken
  stock

½ cup white wine
salt and white pepper to taste
2 tablespoons fresh chives,
  chopped

- Blanch spinach in boiling water until limp (about 1 minute). Immediately place into bowl of ice water. Remove and place on towel and dry well.
- Spread out spinach in a large thin layer in a square shape on a large piece of foil or plastic wrap.

Mousse:

Puree lobster tail meat in food processor or blender. Add cream slowly until well blended.

- Mix in chopped herbs. Season to taste.
- Using a thin spatula, spread mixture in an even layer over the spinach. Roll spinach so that when cut it will have a spiral look.
- Secure in the plastic wrap or foil. Poach or steam in a shallow water bath, covered, for 15-20 minutes in a 375° oven. Cut to serve.

Sauce:

- Boil all sauce ingredients except chives until reduced to 2 cups. Puree in blender or processor.
- Strain and add chives.
- To serve, place sauce on serving plate and lay slices of spinach roll onto sauce, allowing 2-3 slices per serving.
  Serves 4.

Thank you to the Scottsdale Conference Center
for sharing this recipe with us.

Red and White Lobster Mousse

4 Maine lobsters, 1½ pounds
  each
1 quart heavy cream

2 ounces fresh tarragon,
  chopped
salt and pepper
Juice of 2 lemons

Mayonnaise Lobster Sauce:
3 carrots, chopped
6 stalks of celery, chopped

salt and pepper
1 cup mayonnaise

- Boil lobsters for 7 minutes. Remove meat from shells and save. Peel the red part of the meat and add to food processor. Process for 1 minute.
- Add 2 cups of heavy cream. Season with salt, pepper and lemon juice. Add 1 ounce tarragon. Blend until smooth. Remove from processor.
- Add white meat and repeat the same process as with the red meat.
- Layer red and white meat in your favorite pate mold. Chill for 1½ hours. Cut in thin slices. Spoon sauce over top.

Mayonnaise Lobster Sauce:
- Sauté lobster shells in a heavy skillet with carrots and celery. Season with salt and pepper. Add water to cover shells. Boil 1 hour and 15 minutes. Strain.
- Chill liquid. Add to mayonnaise. Spoon over the lobster mousse. **Serves 6.**

Special thanks to the Golden Swan
at the Hyatt Regency Scottsdale
and Executive Chef Anton Brunbauer.

Wonderful accompaniment to roasted veal.

Rib Eye with Texas Chainsaw Chili Sauce

¾ pound beef
½ onion
2 tablespoons garlic
1 carrot
2 cups pureed tomatillos,
  peeled
2 green chilies, roasted and
  remove skin
½ green pepper, roasted and
  remove skin
¼ pound black beans,
  completely cooked
¼ green pepper, diced
¼ red pepper, diced
¼ yellow pepper, diced
½ cup ketchup
2 tablespoons Worchestershire
  sauce

1 tablespoon Tabasco
2 tablespoons tomato paste
2-4 tablespoons dry chili
  powder
1 tablespoon cumin
1 tablespoon coriander
1½ teaspoons ginger
1½ teaspoons white pepper
1½ teaspoons paprika
3 teaspoons cayenne
salt and pepper to taste
molasses, to sweeten, if
  necessary
4 rib eye steaks (8 ounces
  each)
½ cup butter
8 cups veal stock
8 cups chicken stock

- Sear the beef. Brown the vegetables in the same pan. Add tomato paste and caramelize. Add remaining ingredients, except for steaks, butter, flour, veal and chicken stocks.
- Heat veal and chicken stocks.
- In a clean saucepan, blend flour into the butter. Stir over moderate heat until it foams together for two minutes without coloring more than a buttery yellow. Remove from heat.
- When the roux has stopped bubbling, pour into hot stock, whisking vigorously to blend.
- Combine with beef and vegetable mixture.
- Simmer 1 hour, adjusting seasonings.
- Season and grill rib eye steaks. Spoon Chainsaw Chili Sauce over steak. Serve with grilled vegetables, if desired.
  Serves 4.

Special thanks to RoxSand Scocos
of RoxSand Transcontinental Cuisine.

Blueberry Tamale with Mexican Crema

½ cup fresh blueberry puree
(recipe below)
¼ cup sugar
⅛ cup water
1 tablespoon butter
½ cup blue corn masa harina
2 teaspoons molasses

1 cup fresh blueberries
4 dried corn husks
½ cup sour cream
¼ cup whipping cream
2 drops vanilla extract
1 tablespoon Kahlúa

Blue cornmeal masa harina can be replaced by yellow cornmeal. Chef Tozer also recommends using other fresh fruits such as raspberries, rhubarb, peaches, and papaya.

Blueberry Puree:
- Clean and rinse blueberries. In a small saucepan, cook with 1 tablespoon of water and a little sugar, until blueberries are soft. Puree in a blender and pass through a fine sieve. Cool.

Masa Filling:
- Bring puree, water, sugar and molasses to a boil. Whisk in the masa harina and stir over low heat for ten minutes.
- Stir in the butter. Remove from heat.

Corn husks:
- Soak in hot water for 30 minutes or until pliable.
- Lay out husks, opened up. Divide blueberry masa mixture evenly between them. Spread mixture covering the corn husk.
- In the center of each place a teaspoon of fresh blueberries. Fold corn husks over to form a tamale. Fold large end of tamale underneath itself and seal top by tying it with a strip of unused corn husk.
- Steam for 15 minutes. Let rest for 20 minutes.

Mexican Crema:
- Whip sour cream, whipping cream, vanilla and Kahlúa together until it forms soft peaks.

To serve:
- Place warm tamale on a plate. Cut down center from bottom of tamale ¾ of the way up. Pull tamale apart at the bottom and add Mexican Crema.

Serves 4.

***Thanks go to Chef Ian Tozer of the La Hacienda
at the Scottsdale Princess Resort.***

Nougat Glaciers

Nougat:
1 cup + 1 tablespoon sugar
water to dissolve sugar for
  caramelization

5.5 ounces almonds, diced
2 ounces pistachios

Glacier:
2¼ cups cream
3 egg whites

½ cup sugar

Nougat:
- Rub salad oil onto a cookie sheet.
- Spread nuts evenly over sheet.
- Pour caramel over the nuts. Stir with a wooden spoon until stiff.
- Turn out the nougat onto a cutting board. Chop into small pieces.
- Sieve the nougat and discard the powder.

Glacier:
- Whip cream to stiff peaks. Set aside in the refrigerator.
- Dissolve sugar with enough water to cook. Bring sugar to 130° centigrade.
- When sugar boils clear, start whipping the egg whites to stiff peaks.
- While whipping, pour the hot syrup into the egg whites in a steady thin stream. Whip now until the bowl is cool to touch.
- Fold cream and nougat together with the meringue. Be careful not to overfold, as it will break-down the cream.
- Spray a terrine or 6 mousse molds with non-stick. Cover the bottom with some mixture. Tap the terrine sharply on your counter top. Add more mixture and repeat these steps until the terrine is full.
- Freeze terrine for 24 hours. To unmold, soak in sink of hot water so the sides will release. Place into freezer until sides re-refreeze.
- Slice with a serrated knife and serve with fresh berries. Garnish with mint.
Serves 6.

A special thank you to Chef Christopher Gross of Christopher's for sharing this recipe with us.

Desert Melon Soup

2 cups cantaloupe, diced
2 cups honeydew, diced
2 cups prickly pear, diced

squeeze of lemon
dash of heavy cream
Saguaro honey, to taste

Excellent served with the Barbecue Salmon.

- Puree each fruit separately with lemon.
- Lightly whip with cream. Add honey.
- Evenly divide the soup in the same bowl. Garnish with melon of each kind, and place a dab of cream in the center.
  Serves 4.

Thank you to Executive Chef Anton Brunbauer
at the Squash Blossom
at the Hyatt Regency Scottsdale.

Acknowledgements

DEDICATIONS

The Junior League of Phoenix would like to thank these members and friends for financial contributions in support of *Desert Treasures:*

Roberta and Ralph Helm

Gayle Holmgren
To honor the Cookbook Development Committee

Susie and Les Small
To honor Bruce, Scott, Tim and Sarah Small

Ann Denk
To honor her mother, Betty Kitchell

Fund-raising Council 1990-91
To honor Keven Matthew, Fund-raising Council Director
of 1990-91

Gail Creasman
To honor her mother, Joyce Aker

Michelle Felker
To honor her mother, Gerda Hamilton

Charlie and Beth Carson
To honor Mary D. Strauss and Phyliss P. Carson

Keven Matthew
To honor Cookbook co-chairmen, Rebecca Baker and Susie
Wisz for all
their work producing the cookbook.

Nancy Fournier
Dedicated to her children, Catharine and Jacques Fournier

Rae Lynne Chornenky
Dedicated to Gael N. Parks, Betsy Delaney, and Rita
Dickinson

Mrs. Allen R. Austin
Dedicated to Elizabeth Jeffers Porter

Rebecca Baker
Dedicated to Marilyn C. Sayles

Charlie, Woody and Scott Thompson
Dedicated to Kay Thompson, the best wife, mother and
Junior Leaguer. We love you.

Susie Wisz
Dedicated to a superb Cookbook Committee; this book was
a true volunteer effort.

Jennifer Evelyn Sands
In memory of Mr. and Mrs. Henry William Fowler Usher

Mrs. Sanford G. Babson
In memory of her mother, Josephine T. Merkel

Jacquie Dorrance, Sherrie Hackett and Carol Torrey
In memory of Ann Hays Daley

Mr. and Mrs. Edwin Q. Barbey
In memory of Mr. and Mrs. Walter M. Diener

Lyn Fairfax
In memory of Harry and Mabel Manfield

Polly Fitz-Gerald
In memory of Robert L. Bayless, IV

ADDITIONAL
COOKBOOK COMMITTEE

Laurie Airth-Shields	Loris Lynch
Helen Calhoun	Jodie McKenzie
Holly Caldwell*	Debbie Martinez
Jacque Chilton*	Vicki McKellar*
Vicki Clabby	Ann Morris-Hauser
Susan Clayton	Alice Meyer
Kathleen Cohn	Cathy Mullan*
Lynn Donahue*	Diane Norris*
Penne Francis	Holly Peterson
Andrea Katsenes	Joan Puddy*
Kathy Kelty	Karen Rapp
Sharin Feffer*	Susan Refsnes
Julia Fournier	Jill Roberts
Nancy Fournier	Cheryl Schreiner
Patty Hampton-Tzineff	Andrea Smith
Jane Helm	Eden Sommerhalter
Linnea Heitzman	Sue Southwick
Brenda Heurring	Kelli York
Martha Lee*	Jennifer Zweifel

*Indicates members who have
served on this committee for
two years.

The Junior League of Phoenix would like to thank these women who taste tested hundreds of recipies to eliminate all but the very best for *Desert Treasures:*

Chaunci Aeed
Nicia Anderson
Vicki Beaver
Carolyn Board
Sue Bruecher
Shady Calfee
Anita Calihan
Charlie Carson
Betty Cauble
Betsy Delaney
Rita Dickinson
Marsha Dyer
Ann Engle
Bonnie Ewing
Shari Feffer
Margaret Ann Fratt
Pam Gieringer
Diane Goldwater
Betsy Haenel
Eileen Haga
Susan Hagenah
Tony Harper
Sue Harris
Linnea Heitzman
Mary Hudak
Suzi Iliff
Barbara Ireland

Mary Knoll
Barb Kober
Julie Krikac
Martha Lee
Terri Luke
Cheryl Levinson
Vickie McKellar
Mary Sue Magura
Terry Mainwaring
Sue Marovick
Beth Matthews
Rita Michalko
Kim Myers
Claudia Neal
Diane Norris
Susie Osborn
Gael Parks
Jane Polacek
Kathy Povepore
Cay Rasor
Caren Cowie-Redivo
Michael Register
Jill Roberts
Susan Rose
Jane Russell
Lois Savage
Ann Scardello

Judy Schubert
Judy Shannon
Kathy Shook
Connie Siever
Andrea Smith
Joan Smith
Anne Sterling
Kim Sterling
Joan Strand
Sue Southwick
Anne Spellman
Sandy Thomas
Linda Thompson
Val Thompson
Kris Vandenburg
Julie Van Drunen
Sarah Weissinger
Nancy Whit
Karen Vivian
Susie Wesley
Nancy White
Barby Corbet Woods
Deedie Wrigley
Danette Wurtz
Anne Yearley
Diane Young
Deborah Zack

The Junior League of Phoenix would like to thank its members, their families and friends who supported this project by contributing recipes.

Claire Able
Chaunci Aeed
Adrienne Bridgewater Anderson
Janet Arnold, Jr.
Millie Arnold
Naomi Asta
Becky Babson
Amy Bacal
Ann Barker
Mark Barker
Sandra Barnes
Katie Barrette
Kathy Bates
Ann Beardsley
Mary Jo Beardsley
T. J. Bedard
Chris Benscotter
Kay Berry
Emily Blount
Carolyn Board
Evonne Bowling
Cynthia Bracken
Carol Brookes
Susan Brown
Laura Brownfield
Royce Brownfield
Annie Burton
Jan Cacheris
Shady Calfee
Anita Calihan
Karen Campbell
Charlie Carson
Patti Carter
Betty Cauble
Kim Cerchiai
Rae Chornenky
Zipper Clark
Barbara Cockle
Colleen Cookson
Debbie Coor
Tibby Cornelius
Virginia Crabb
Gail Creasman
Josephine Cumins
Char Davis
Linda Day

Sharon Day
Becki Deem
Lorena DeHanas
Rita Dickinson
Cheryl Dolph-Karlsson
Mary Ducharme
Nancy Skiles Dunlap
Marsha Dyer
Margi Edlund
Janet Edmonds
Alexander Elsner
Winifred Erickson
Lyn Fairfax
Shari Feffer
Michelle Felker
Janet Finch
Tami Fitzgerald
Melinda Foote
Shannon Forseth
Nancy Fournier
Dawn Fouts
Regina Gabbert
Pamela J. Gieringer
Melissa Goett
Bob Goldwater
Diane Goldwater
Vicki Granberry
Karen Green
Susie Groff
Janie Grue
Kathleen Hadd
Betsy Haenel
Ginny Haenel
Susan Hagenah
Susan Hall
Suzanne Hansen
Linda Harland
Sandi Harrington
Sue Harris
Beryl Hassig
Ann Morris Hauser
Lund Hedges
Linnea Heitzman
Jane Helm
Michele Hershfield
Brenda Heuring
Jean Hickey
Linda Higgins
Michelle Hirshfield
Gayle Holmgren
Mary Hudak
Jan Hutchison
Suzi Iliff

Barbara Ireland
Lucy Jackson
Jean Jani
Stacey Jani
Dana Jirauch
Maeve Johnson
Susan Davenport Johnson
Beverly Jones
Marianne Jones
Susan V. Jones
Robyn Julien
Barbara Junior
Mary Jane Whitaker Karr
Rona Kasen
Susan Kaufman
Lynn Ketelsen
Pauline King
Robin Kline
Mary Knoll
Barb Kober
Margaret Kober
Sandra Koberstein
Ann Kunkel
Holly Larsen
Marci Larsen
Martha Lee
Deborah Lemos
Cheryl Levinson
Tammy Linn
Cindy List
Fleur Long
Terri Luke
Irene Lundahl
Mary Lou Lyding
Carol Maes
Georgia Magoun
Dr. Donna Manzelmann
Susan Marovic
Keven Matthew
Beth Matthews
Faith McLoon
Marjane McDougall
Mary Helen McGinn
Vicki McKellar
Joanne Menapace
Priscilla Miller
Robin Milne
Carole Moreno
Carla Moring
Kim Myers
Mary Navarro
Claudia Neal
Betty Norris

Debbie Norris
Diane Norris
Nan Nygaard
Gail Gordon Ober
Grace O'choa
Joanie O'Connor
Rachel Osterle
Pam Olmstead
Susi Osborn
Betty Olwin
Hazel Paisley
Gael Parks
Marlene Pawlowski
Joyce Lynn Pedrotti
Jo-Em Perkins
Stacey Pilcher
May Powell
Mary Ellen Prosper
Joan Puddy
Plattie Quest
Jane Ramsland
Cay Rasor
Christine Reeves
Michael Regester
Judy Rieckhoff
Kathy Ringwald
Nancy Roach
Connie Rodie
Rebecca Rodie
Robin Rodie
Marguerite Roll
Betsy Rominger
Mrs. Elliott Roosevelt
Barb Rose
Erika Rothermel
Diane Rousseau
Randi Rummage
Jane Russell
Joan Ryan
Sharron Saffert
Diane Sander
Jennifer Sands
Lois Savage
Ann Scardello
Carol Schmidt
Judy Schubert
Kathy Seid
Bobbie Sferra
Judy Shannon
Beverly Shaver
Cherri Sheely
Alma Shelly
Joan Shepherd

Genie Rankin Sherard
Jackie Sherwood
Kelly Sifferman
Joan Smith
Kathy Smith
Lee Smith
M. Smith
Sylvia Smith
Marron Snead
Vera Soltau
Sue Southwick
Anne Spellman
Suzan Spiekerman
Sally Stead
Jacque Steiner
J. Stewart
Meredith Hoff Stewart
Anne Sterling
Joan Stand
Mary Stull
Pam Sturgeon
Betty Lou Summers
Keri Sweet
Susan Tanita
Linda Teichgraeber
Carolyn Thomas
Jane Thurwachter
Judy Tierney
Barbara Todd
Harriet Van B.
Julie VanDrunen
Kelley Vieregg
Karen Vivian
Marlene Walter
Chris Wertheim
Dana Westphal
Lyn Wiley
Fiora Williams
June Williams
Karren Williams
Libby Williams
Gretchen Wilson
Shirley Winslow
Susie Wisz
Peggy Withers
Suzanne Wood
Irene Woodhead
Barby Corbet Woods
Deedie Wrigley
Danette Wurtz
Anne Yearley
Diane Young
Deborah Zack

Index

DESERT TREASURES Order Form

Name _____

Address _____

City _____ State _____ Zip _____ Telephone (____) _____

Please send me _____ copies of *Desert Treasures* at $18.95 each = $ _____

Plus $2.50 shipping and handling ($5.00 for orders of 2 or more) = $ _____

TOTAL = $ _____

Please charge my: ( ) VISA or ( ) Mastercard

Card number _____

Expiration date _____

Cardholder's
Signature _____

Please make checks payable to:

The Junior League of Phoenix

Please do not send cash. Sorry, no C.O.D.'s.

Mail to: *Desert Treasures*
The Junior League of Phoenix, Inc.
PO Box 10223, Phoenix, AZ 85064
(602) 230-9573

Profits from the sale of Desert Treasures are used to support the purpose and programs of The Junior League of Phoenix, Inc.

- -

DESERT TREASURES Order Form

Name _____

Address _____

City _____ State _____ Zip _____ Telephone (____) _____

Please send me _____ copies of *Desert Treasures* at $18.95 each = $ _____

Plus $2.50 shipping and handling ($5.00 for orders of 2 or more) = $ _____

TOTAL = $ _____

Please charge my: ( ) VISA or ( ) Mastercard

Card number _____

Expiration date _____

Cardholder's
Signature _____

Please make checks payable to:

The Junior League of Phoenix

Please do not send cash. Sorry, no C.O.D.'s.

Mail to: *Desert Treasures*
The Junior League of Phoenix, Inc.
PO Box 10223, Phoenix, AZ 85064
(602) 230-9573

Profits from the sale of Desert Treasures are used to support the purpose and programs of The Junior League of Phoenix, Inc.

- -

DESERT TREASURES Order Form

Name _____

Address _____

City _____ State _____ Zip _____ Telephone (____) _____

Please send me _____ copies of *Desert Treasures* at $18.95 each = $ _____

Plus $2.50 shipping and handling ($5.00 for orders of 2 or more) = $ _____

TOTAL = $ _____

Please charge my: ( ) VISA or ( ) Mastercard

Card number _____

Expiration date _____

Cardholder's
Signature _____

Please make checks payable to:

The Junior League of Phoenix

Please do not send cash. Sorry, no C.O.D.'s.

Mail to: *Desert Treasures*
The Junior League of Phoenix, Inc.
PO Box 10223, Phoenix, AZ 85064
(602) 230-9573

Profits from the sale of Desert Treasures are used to support the purpose and programs of The Junior League of Phoenix, Inc.